COINS AND THE BIBLE

Richard Abdy & Amelia Dowler

THE
BRITISH
MUSEUM

SPINK
FOUNDED 1666

© Richard Abdy and Amelia Dowler 2013
Published in conjunction with the exhibition *Coins and the Bible,*
Organised by The Department of Coins and Medals, The British Museum
London, 17 May - 20 October, 2013
The exhibition is supported by Howard and Roberta Ahmanson

Typesetting and Layout by Russell Whittle
Printed and bound by in Malta
by Gutenberg Press Ltd.

for the publishers
Spink & Son Ltd., 69 Southampton Row
Bloomsbury, London, WC1B 4ET, UK
www.spink.com

ISBN 978-1-907427-30-5

Cover illustrations: (Front) 'Thirty Pieces of Silver' (see fig. 2.9); fragment of papyrus
(Book of Revelation, see fig. 6.4). (Back) Hinton St. Mary Mosaic (see fig. 7.22)

CONTENTS

Acknowledgements

Donal Bateson

Andrea Clarke

Felicity Cobbing

Chris Entwistle

Catherine Eagleton

Haim Gitler

Amanda Gregory

Simon James

Scot McKendrick

Maria Cristina Molinari

Elisabeth O'Connell

Rebecca Penrose

Philip Skingley

Jonathan Tubb

Sam Moorhead

Jonathan Williams

Conservation by Pippa Pearce and Duygu Camurcuoglu

Photography by Saul Peckham and Stephen Dodd

Design by Russell Whittle

FOREWORD

About a third of the world's population are Christians; several billion copies of the Bible have been printed over time. Even before the modern period and the advent of printing, the Old and New Testaments must have been, as they still are, among the best, if not the best, known texts throughout the world, past and present.

The coins mentioned in the Bible have exercised a mesmeric and sometimes spiritual fascination over time. The "widow's mite" and the "tribute penny" are well known, but probably the most famous were the thirty pieces of silver, for which Judas Iscariot betrayed Jesus. They were well known in the Middle Ages, and some sources purported to give the 'long history' of such coins, going well back into Old Testament times. The stories were known in medieval England also, and in the fourteenth century an anonymous poet described how

For thritty pens thai solden that childe; the seller highth Judas
(for thirty pence they sold that child; the seller was called Judas).

Coins thought to be some of the original 30 pieces often found their way into church treasuries. Some 15-20, at least, survived into modern times, sadly (in one sense) mostly being something else: most often ancient silver coins of the Mediterranean island of Rhodes. Such coins were known to travellers in the Levant, and bear a radiate head of the sun god Helios which may have been taken to represent Christ with a crown of thorns.

People started to collect coins in the early days of the European Renaissance, and from then there has been a special interest in Biblical such coins, and indeed they have been faked since that time (since they have always been valued at a premium over other coins). Perhaps the first serious study was made by Heinrich Bünting, a German protestant pastor and theologian, who mapped out the geography of the Bible lands in his *Itinerarium Sacrae Scripturae*, first published in Helmstedt in 1582. It included a section *De monetis et mensuris Sacrae Scripturae* (Concerning the coins and measuring standards of the Holy Scriptures), more fully described as follows, translated from the German:

A true calculation and description of all coins and weights in the holy Scripture. Therein all silver and gold coins, and all corn and wine measures of the Hebrews, Greeks and Romans, as many of which are mentioned in the Old and New Testaments are duly explained, and are compared with our coins and weights, calculated and drawn together from books which have been consulted.

The book became very popular, and, in the seventeenth century, it was translated into English, and editions were printed in London several times, in 1619, 1623, 1629, 1636 and 1682, thus testifying to the fascination generated by its contents. Interestingly, the English version was adapted for its new readership (just as many of the coin terms in the Bible itself had been 'translated' for its original, non-Levantine audience): 'also a short treatise of the weights, monies, and measures mentioned in the Scriptures, reduced to our English valuations, quantitie and weight'.

Not long after, the first book to be devoted solely to the topic was published, Kaspar Waser's *De antiquis numis Hebraeorum, Chaldaeorum et Syrorum, quorum S. Biblia Rabbinorum scripta meminerunt* (Concerning the ancient coins of the Hebrews, Chaldaeans and Syrians, which the Holy Bible and Rabbinic writings mention). First published in Zurich in 1605, it too became a popular book, reprinted several times subsequently, including one edition published for a British audience in London in 1660.

Since then many other scholars have treated the topic. Augustin Calmet's great *Dictionnaire .... de la Bible*, published in French in the early 18th century and translated in to English as soon as 1732 included 'a dissertation upon Jewish coins and medals'. But it was the slightly later work of Francis Perez Bayer, *De numis Hebraeo-Samaratanis* (Valencia, 1781) which really established the topic. Little of great importance was subsequently published until a flurry of activity in the middle of the nineteenth century, which saw first C. Cavedoni's *Numismatica Biblica* (Modena, 1850), then F. De Saulcy's *Recherches sur la numismatique judaique* (Paris, 1854), and finally the work of Frederic Madden of the British Museum. 'Young Madden', as he is still known to distinguish him from his more famous father (who was the museum's Keeper of Manuscripts), had a somewhat chequered career at the museum, being 'for a short time a curator in the Department of Coins & Medals but was obliged to resign following a 'misunderstanding' over the sale of duplicates' (as it is delicately put) in 1868. His *History of Jewish Coinage, and of Money in the Old and New Testament* was first published almost 150 years ago, in 1864, and remained a standard work for over a century, and the foundation of modern 'scientific' studies.

Thus the strong link between the British Museum and Biblical numismatics was firmly established, and the tradition was later continued in the early twentieth century by Sir George Hill, Keeper of Coins and later Director of the Museum. His extraordinary grasp of history and languages enabled him to publish many of the volumes of the *British Museum Catalogue of Greek Coins*, including the volume on *Palestine* in 1914. The book catalogued what was the probably the best collection in the world, since in 1908 Hill had managed to acquire the coins belonging to Leopold Hamburger, a Jerusalem banker, after he was declared bankrupt. Hamburger's coins remain the backbone of the museum's collection, although some important acquisitions have been made over the last hundred years, and indeed some of the subsequent curators have continued to write on Biblical subjects (as indeed this book itself). Over the last 60 years a great tradition of study has, unsurprisingly, grown up also in Israel, led by the indefatigable Ya'akov Meshorer. Great collections have been and are being formed in many parts of the world, especially there and in the USA, and the topic now has a truly world-wide following.

Today, indeed, interest in the topic continues unabated; hardly a year goes by without another volume being published, whether academic or more popular, and every Christmas and Easter is marked by a marketing campaign by those who sell reproductions of Biblical coins. Thanks to the generosity of Howard and Roberta Ahmanson, the British Museum is showing the exhibition which this book accompanies in 2013, the anniversary of the so-called Edict of Milan, when the Roman emperor Constantine permitted people of the Christian faith to practise their beliefs without persecution, thus paving the way for the establishment of Christianity as an official state religion, and its subsequent rise as one of the world's great faiths.

Andrew Burnett

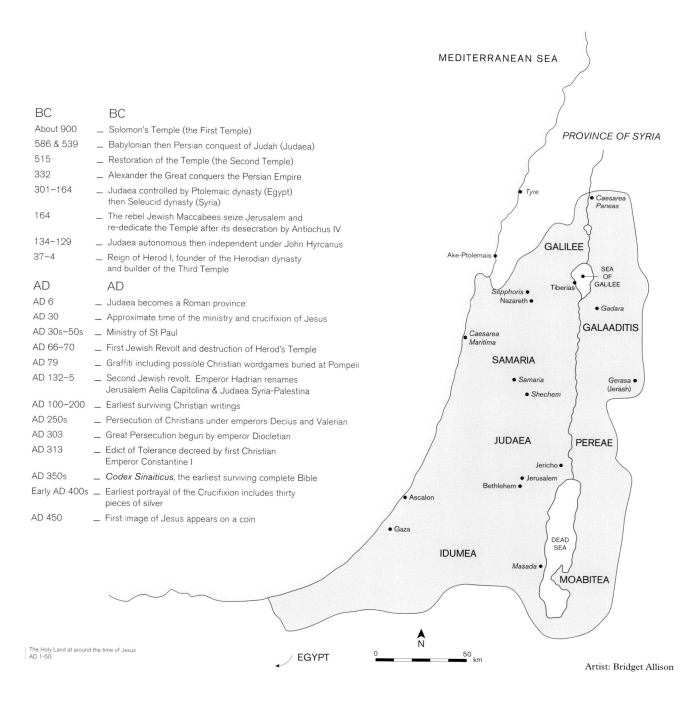

BC

BC	
About 900	— Solomon's Temple (the First Temple)
586 & 539	— Babylonian then Persian conquest of Judah (Judaea)
515	— Restoration of the Temple (the Second Temple)
332	— Alexander the Great conquers the Persian Empire
301–164	— Judaea controlled by Ptolemaic dynasty (Egypt) then Seleucid dynasty (Syria)
164	— The rebel Jewish Maccabees seize Jerusalem and re-dedicate the Temple after its desecration by Antiochus IV
134–129	— Judaea autonomous then independent under John Hyrcanus
37–4	— Reign of Herod I, founder of the Herodian dynasty and builder of the Third Temple

AD

AD	
AD 6	— Judaea becomes a Roman province
AD 30	— Approximate time of the ministry and crucifixion of Jesus
AD 30s–50s	— Ministry of St Paul
AD 66–70	— First Jewish Revolt and destruction of Herod's Temple
AD 79	— Graffiti including possible Christian wordgames buried at Pompeii
AD 132–5	— Second Jewish revolt. Emperor Hadrian renames Jerusalem Aelia Capitolina & Judaea Syria-Palestina
AD 100–200	— Earliest surviving Christian writings
AD 250s	— Persecution of Christians under emperors Decius and Valerian
AD 303	— Great Persecution begun by emperor Diocletian
AD 313	— Edict of Tolerance decreed by first Christian Emperor Constantine I
AD 350s	— *Codex Sinaiticus*, the earliest surviving complete Bible
Early AD 400s	— Earliest portrayal of the Crucifixion includes thirty pieces of silver
AD 450	— First image of Jesus appears on a coin

MEDITERRANEAN SEA

PROVINCE OF SYRIA

Tyre

Caesarea Paneas

GALILEE

Ake-Ptolemais

SEA OF GALILEE

Sepphoris

Tiberias

Nazareth

Gadara

GALAADITIS

Caesarea Maritima

SAMARIA

Samaria

Gerasa (Jerash)

Shechem

JUDAEA

PEREAE

Jericho

Jerusalem

Bethlehem

Ascalon

Gaza

DEAD SEA

IDUMEA

Masada

MOABITEA

The Holy Land at around the time of Jesus
AD 1-50

N

EGYPT

0   50
km

Artist: Bridget Allison

Chapter One

MONEY AND THE OLD TESTAMENT (EARLY BEGINNINGS TO 332 BC)

The World of the Old Testament

The Old Testament, or Hebrew Bible, comprises the first and larger part of the Christian Bible and is a collection of writings composed over a long period detailing the origins and history of the people and land of Israel. Exactly what is included in the Old Testament differs between Christian denominations. In the Roman Catholic and Orthodox churches a higher number of Old Testament books are used and these are often referred to as the Apocrypha in the Protestant tradition where they are either included as a separate, less authoritative, section between the Old and New Testaments or not included at all. Even in the Catholic tradition where they are integrated amongst the books of the Old Testament, the books of the Apocrypha are referred to as 'deuterocanonical', which theoretically at least means that they have a lower status than the other books of the Old Testament. In practice however, they are treated as part of the Old Testament.

When the Old Testament was set down is open to debate. Originally it was thought that its composition extended over a thousand years from the Song of Moses (Exodus 15) and the Song of Deborah (Judges 5) to the final work, the Book of Daniel. This would cover the 11th/10th Century BC to the 2nd Century BC and if one included the Apocrypha this would extend to the 1st Century BC (The Wisdom of Solomon). References to the Temple in the Song of Moses however have suggested to many modern scholars that it may have been written later. The Temple of Solomon was thought to have been built in the 10th Century BC although it was probably constructed later and ascribed to the famous king. It is very likely that much of the Old Testament reached its present form in the Persian period (538-332BC). No matter when the first books of the Old Testament were first written however it is clear that the writing extended over a very long period in comparison with the New Testament. This long period saw many political and cultural changes in the Holy Land and these are reflected in the Old Testament.

Though there are plenty of references in the Old Testament to trade, exchange, and measurements, coinage was not in existence for much of the period covered by the text. In the Mediterranean world coinage was first used in Asia Minor, now Turkey, from the 7th century BC onwards and the concept spread very rapidly thereafter, particularly amongst Greek city states. By the 5th century BC coins were used widely across the whole Mediterranean and silver was the most popular metal used for striking coins. The striking of copper alloy coins, such as bronze, was not very widespread until the Hellenistic period after the death of Alexander the Great of Macedon in 323BC. By the time the Romans were dominant in the Holy Land, from the 1st century BC, the use of copper alloy coinage was extensive.

The Shekel system: Weights and Measures

Like many ancient coinage systems, the coins used in the Holy Land developed from systems of weights and measures. This is true of many currencies still used today – the pound, for example. The term 'shekel', later used to describe coins, originally referred to a measure of weight and the word

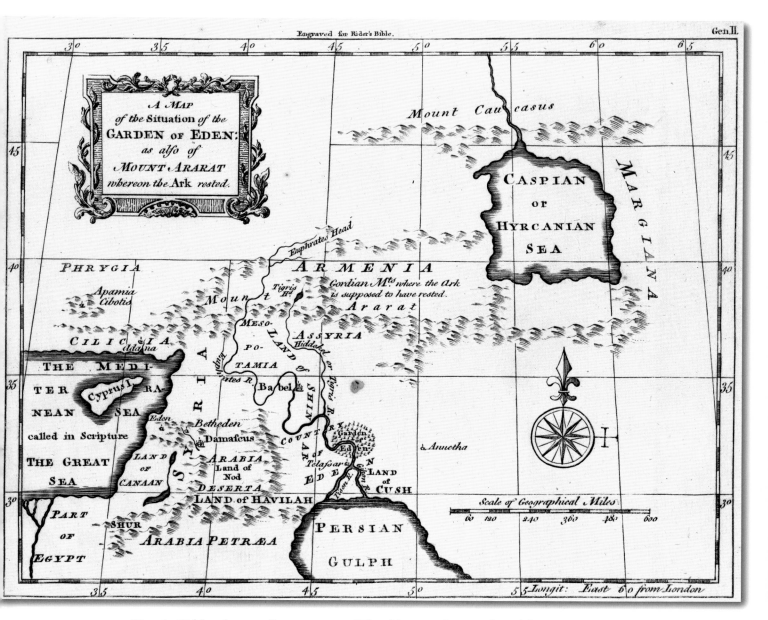

Fig. 1: Biblical map illustration to 'The Christian's Family Bible' (1763-67)

itself derives from the Hebrew for 'weighing' and was also used as a weight term in Akkadian, a Mesopotamian language. Though the shekel was used as a unit of weight for hundreds of years across a very wide area the exact weight of the shekel varied depending on where the transaction took place and between whom.

As with similar terms used elsewhere, different weight standards could apply to a weight described as a 'shekel' and this would often be clarified in the text describing the transaction:

four hundred shekels of silver, according to the weight current among the merchants. (Genesis 23:16)

The total amount of the gold from the wave offering[1] used for all the work on the sanctuary was 29 talents and 730 shekels, according to the sanctuary shekel. (Exodus 38:24)

This did not only apply to precious metals:

500 shekels of cassia—all according to the sanctuary shekel— and a hin of olive oil. (Exodus 30:24)

Fig. 2

The standard is not always mentioned and so we can only assume must have been understood in the context of the transaction (geographical or otherwise). This meant that the exact weight of the shekel could change as would the subdivisions. The Canaanite/Israelite shekel, probably the 'sacred' or sanctuary standard referred to above, was 11.40g, for example, but the Babylonian shekel was 8.70g.

The shekel was used in many different communities. In Babylon for example the Stele of Nabonidus [fig. 2] from c. 555-539BC celebrates the return of abundance the land after a drought listing how the prices of goods, measured in shekels (šiklu) of silver have risen. Though here shekels of silver are used to measure prices it is clear that these terms were often used as accounting devices and prices paid (or goods exchanged) may have been other items. Still earlier in Babylon this method of accounting and exchange can be seen on the stone kudurru known as 'The Establisher of the Boundary Forever' from the reign of Marduk-nadin-ahhe (1099-1082 BC) [fig. 3]. The boundary stone records a land sale where the value is given in silver, but was paid in various forms – a chariot, saddles, two asses, an ox, grain, oil, and certain garments, the items being separately valued and making a total of seven hundred and sixteen shekels of silver.

Weights used for measurements in this system were made from a variety of materials and shapes and apart from inscriptions give some of the earliest indications of the use of shekels as a unit of weight. Though meant for practical usage, weights could be very decorative, such as those made from agate in the form of frogs or ducks. Clearly the

Fig. 3

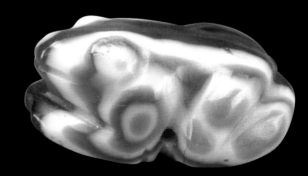

Fig. 4

same methods and practices were in use for a long period ranging from an Akkadian agate frog of 2400-2200BC [fig. 4] to the Babylonian agate ducks of 700-500BC [fig. 5] and beyond. All these seem to be crafted to cater to the local shekel weight systems and as well as the shekel unit itself also provided for subdivisions and multiples. The duck weights pictured range from one to three Babylonian shekels, for example. The use of the word 'shekel' in inscriptions begins only a little later than this in the late 3rd millennium BC and thereafter is used widely as a unit of measurement in the Middle East.

Weights for measuring Canaanite/Israelite shekels were mainly made from polished limestone, which could be engraved with the name of the weight in Egyptian hieratic script or Hebrew.

Fig. 5

Fig. 6

A number of these have been found at excavations at Lachish, south-west of Jerusalem. Shekel weights were usually rendered as a single shekel (and lower subdivisions) and then in multiples of two and the largest weight in the Lachish group is an 8 shekel weight. The shekel came after the talent and mina in the weight system used in the eastern Mediterranean (except Egypt, which had its own systems). The exact number of minas to the talent and shekels to the mina could also vary across localities.

Canaanite/Israelite Weights[2]:

	Weight	Per Talent	Per Mina	Per Shekel
Talent	34.2kg	1	–	–
Mina	5.70kg	60	1	–
Shekel	11.40g	3,000	50	1
Nezef	9.12g	3,750	62.5	5/6
Pym	7.60g	4,500	75	2/3
Beka	5.70g	6,000	100	2
Gerah (20)	0.57g	60,000	1,000	20
Gerah (24)	0.48g	71,250	1,187.5	24

The smallest division, the gerah (also the Akkadian word for a carob seed), appears to vary between 20 and 24 to the shekel depending on the weight standard used. Biblical references specifically mention 20 gerot to the shekel on the sacred standard and this has been interpreted to mean that there was another number of gerot to the shekel under other standards. Most importantly it appears that once coins are introduced, there are 24 gerot to the shekel. Beforehand however it is clear that there were 20 gerot to the shekel:

The shekel is to consist of twenty gerahs. Twenty shekels plus twenty-five shekels plus fifteen shekels equal one mina. (Ezekial 45:12)

Though the use of silver weighed in shekels was often simply an accounting device it is clear that there was also a widespread silver trade throughout the Eastern Mediterranean and Middle East. Silver ingots, for example from Zincirli (ancient Sam'al) in modern Turkey, were widely traded. [fig. 7] From c. 730BC, it is inscribed in Aramaic, the main administrative script of the Persian Empire which was used to write down many different languages. Before it was cut down, this ingot probably weighed a mina (or sixty shekels) on the Babylonian standard. As coins were introduced from the 7th century BC onwards, they circulated alongside the ingots in the same trading systems as the important factor was their weight (and metal purity) which meant that coins could be treated in much the same way as ingots in transactions and vice versa. Even when coinage was quite well established, this tradition continued and this silver fragment [fig. 8] comes from a hoard buried in Babylon in the early 4th century BC, which contained various chopped and twisted pieces of silver cut from silver vessels as well as jewellery, amulets and coins. The use of silver and gold in weights, rather than as coins, continued far into New Testament times. Both Matthew and Luke refer to this in their parables of the Talents and the Minas as will be seen in chapter 4. Even though coins were widely used by this period, the concept of measuring silver in weights was still important. Where large weights are specified in the Bible however, it is possible that this weight is made from ingots, coins, or a mixture of ingots and coins, just like the Babylonian hoard.

Fig. 7

Fig. 8

Coin use in Bible lands

The first coins used in the Levant would have been predominantly silver coinages produced by central Greek city states such as Athens [fig. 9] and Aegina, northern Greek city states like Acanthus, and the Thraco-Macedonian tribes. It is possible that these would have been used alongside Persian gold and silver coins (darics and sigloi) which were produced by Achaemenid Persia, in control of the region at this time although these have not been found in local excavations. All these coins were produced from the mid-6th century BC onwards and such incoming coinages were joined by the more local Phoenician silver coins. The first coins to be called shekels were really the Persian sigloi [fig. 10], produced in Asia Minor from the 6th century BC onwards. Siglos is a Greek word derived from the same root as shekel. Following this, Phoenician coins were minted in silver from the 5th century BC onwards. These had very different weight standards – the Persian siglos weight began at 5.35g in the 6th century BC but was raised in the 5th century BC to 5.55g whereas Phoenician coins were based on a shekel unit of about 7g. The Old Testament also records other coin terms – the Daric

Fig. 9

Fig. 10

Fig. 11

for example [fig. 11] is referred to in Chronicles, Ezra and Nehemiah. Here the term appears to be recording large amounts of gold, which suggest that it is being used as a weight or accounting term rather than referring to coins specifically. This is probably the case for many of the shekel references in the Old Testament even after the introduction of coinage in the region.

There was already an extensive silver trading network in the eastern Mediterranean before the use of coinage. From hoard evidence it appears that silver coins have a similar distribution since silver coins and 'hacksilber' (cut up coins and bullion) are found alongside silver ingots in archaic hoards. The main directions of silver travel were from the silver rich mining areas of northern Greece (Mount Pangaion region) and central Greece (predominantly Athens' mine at Laurion) to 'silver-poor' areas in the east (through Levantine ports eastwards to the Middle East, central Asia, and south to Arabia); south (to Egypt); west (to Sicily and Italy). This typical pattern of silver movement accounts for the number of Greek (silver) coins in the Middle East in addition to the coinage of Persia (rulers over much of this area) and Phoenicia (neighbours). The coins of Phoenicia, from mints like Sidon [fig. 12] and Tyre [fig. 13], also circulated widely. From

archaeological data, both Greek and Phoenician coins appear to have been used more frequently than Persian coins, despite the fact that Judah was a Persian province. Since most transactions would still have required the weighing of silver coins (possibly alongside hacksilber or ingots as well) multiple weight standards for these differing systems would not have affected the practicality of accepting many different coin types in the area. It is highly likely also that the various equivalences would have been well known to traders at least.

Fig. 12

Fig. 13

Taking in and loaning out payments in silver was a common function of ancient temples and there is widespread evidence for this in many different areas particularly in Greek temple inventories which survive since they were inscribed in stone. In the Bible, Judges 9:4 records that in Canaanite Shechem the Israelites worshipped Baal-Berith (the Baal or 'god' of the covenant) after the death of Gideon instead of God and it appears that Baal's temple also took in silver as tribute or payments:

They gave him seventy shekels of silver from the temple of Baal-Berith, and Abimelek used it to hire reckless scoundrels, who became his followers. (Judges 9:4)

These shekels again would have been cut pieces of silver rather than coins. It is of interest to note that in Christian demonology Baal-Berith is the demon who incites blasphemy and murder but also can turn any metal into gold.

The first shekel coins were produced in the southern Levant – Philistia and Samaria, and then in Judah and possibly also in Edom – in the 4th century BC. Philistia comprised the Philistine confederacy of the five city-states of Ashkalon, Ashdod, Gaza, Gat and Ekron although only the first three minted coins. The most productive Philistian mint was at Gaza. Samaria and Judah only had single mints at Samaria (later Sebaste) and Jerusalem. They all produced coinages which were based on local shekel weight standards either in divisions of shekels or lower denomination terms such as gerah or ma'ah. Most of these coins are smaller denominations which may suggest that larger silver coins from other areas were still well used in the area for larger transactions. However, these smaller denominations in the weight system used for Temple payments might have facilitated the annual tribute. These early coins were heavily influenced by the arrival of Greek and Phoenician coins in the area. In particular the coinages of Philistia [fig. 14] and Samaria [fig. 15], appear to have early design connections to Greek and Phoenician coins respectively, but take

Fig. 14

Fig. 15

these ideas and reinterpret them in a local context, combining local design motifs with features which may still be traced back to their Greek and Phoenician roots. The coins of Judah, known as the 'Yehud' coins may have initially been produced at the mint of Gaza. 'Yehud' is the Persian name for the province (later known as 'Judaea' under the Roman Empire) and this appears on the coins either as a full inscription (in Aramaic script) YHD or just with the initial Y on smaller coins. Some early examples appear to have the mint mark of Gaza (the Aramaic letter ayin) which has led to the belief that the coins were initially produced in Philistia before production began in Judah itself.

The most famous of these coins is a unique quarter shekel in the British Museum collection [fig. 16]. The inscription on the reverse accompanies a bearded deity seated right on winged chariot, and holding a falcon, and has generally been read as YHD (i.e. 'Yehud' = Judah) but it has also been interpreted as 'YHW' or 'YHR' (i.e. 'Yahweh' = God). This is controversial and engenders considerable academic debate. One suggestion is that as the initial production of this coin series was outside Judah itself (and probably at Gaza, a pagan city) then the normal prohibition of the second commandment might not have been regarded. The seated deity could then be seen as only one deity amongst a vast pantheon existing across the Middle East at this period. Coins of this style continued to be produced after

Fig. 16

333BC when Alexander the Great conquered the Persian Empire and also during the Seleucid and Ptolemaic domination of the area. The seated deity figure was not repeated however. Increasingly, the coinage systems of the Seleucid and Ptolemaic dynasties (based in Syria and Egypt respectively) came to dominate the coin usage of the area and the last locally produced and inspired coins probably came to an end in the 260s BC.

Chapter Two

BETWEEN THE TESTAMENTS: GREEKS AND THE HASMONEANS (332-40 BC)

When Alexander the Great defeated the Persian Empire in the mid-4th century BC, he brought with him new types of coins and varied designs from the Greek world [fig. 1]. From this point onwards, Greek culture had a much wider influence in the Middle East, which had direct implications for the Jews living in Judah and neighbouring areas. After Alexander's death, his coins continued to be produced by his Successors who initially ruled in Alexander's name. The Successors were Alexander's generals and therefore had no immediate blood-tie to the royal family. They fought a series of bloody wars after Alexander's death and it was only at the very end of the 4th century BC that the remaining Successor generals felt secure enough to declare themselves kings in their own right. Judaea was initially controlled by the Seleucid dynasty. The Seleucids were based at first in Babylon and then at a new capital, Seleucia on the Tigris, in Syria. Their neighbours, the Ptolemaic dynasty in Egypt, vied for control over the area as it was strategically important. The Seleucids and Ptolemies fought over the Levant area for many years in a

Fig. 1

series of conflicts known as the Syrian Wars. This meant that the area changed hands frequently. The inland area of Judah was, however, more often in Seleucid control than Ptolemaic. Coins minted in the area included posthumous coins of Alexander minted by his Successors but also at independent mints. These "Alexander" coins were minted across the Eastern Mediterranean down till the 2nd -1st centuries BC and appear to have been used widely in trade [fig. 2]. In the Levant, mints for the coins of Alexander (including posthumous coins), Seleucid and Ptolemaic coins were mainly, Ake-Ptolemais (Akko), Ashkalon, Demetrias ad Mare, Dora, Gaza, Joppa, Samaria and possibly also Jerusalem. These coins were all on Greek (drachm) weight standards. Alexander had adopted the popular Attic weight standard (17.2g for a silver tetradrachm or four drachma piece), which continued to be used by most of his Successors. The Ptolemies however used a reduced standard which dropped from their original Attic usage probably due to the paucity of silver in Egypt. All of these coins were used widely in the area although the use of the reduced weight Ptolemaic coins fluctuated with ptolemaic political influence over the coastal regions of Phoenicia [fig. 3]. The eagle prevalent on Ptolemaic coins heavily influenced the design of the later shekels of independent Tyre and possibly also the Herodian eagle type looked at in the next chapter.

Fig. 2

Fig. 3

The Hasmonean dynasty, emerged during the Maccabean revolts against Seleucid rule, and became fully established as rulers of Judah under John Hyrcanus I (Yehohanan) in 135 as both king and high priest. This dynasty remained in power until the victory of Herod the Great, who founded the Herodian dynasty with Roman support in around 40BC. The Hasmoneans only minted bronze coins, which are typically called a prutah (pl. prutot) – probably what they were called at the time although this term is only recorded later in rabbinical texts for copper alloy coins. The shekel therefore does not appear to have been used as a coin term at this period although no doubt it continued to be used in the local weight systems. This state of affairs continued under the Herodian dynasty and the official Roman coins in the later province of Judaea were also bronze or operated under Roman denomination systems (i.e. denarius for silver). The Roman Procurators in the area also only minted in bronze. The shekel as a coin was produced elsewhere however, most notably at Tyre, and this was of great importance for the annual tribute paid by all observant Jews to the Temple. Silver was also available from neighbouring areas, including Roman mints in Syria.

The Books of the Maccabees are considered differently depending on Christian denomination. For Protestants, the books are either apocryphal (and kept in a separate section) or form no part of the Bible whatsoever but Books I-II of the Maccabees are included as standard in the Old Testament of Catholic Bibles and those of the Orthodox churches. For the latter Books III-IV of the Maccabees are also generally included. I Maccabees was originally written in Hebrew but only a Greek translation survives of the whole text. The further three books were composed in Greek. This is one of the reasons that many Protestant churches do not include the books in the Old Testament since the Protestant canon is based on the Jewish books composed in Hebrew or Aramaic. These books are important however to illustrate the life and times of the people in Judaea immediately before the time of Jesus and demonstrate the political processes at play in state and religious practice. The religious tenets embraced by the Hasmoneans, the dynasty who grew out of the Maccabean Revolt, are illustrated on their coins. The story of the Maccabean martyrs, recounted in II Maccabees and later extolled in IV Maccabees, influenced the foundation of the Christian concept of Martyrdom.

The Maccabees

The story of the Maccabean Revolt, recounted in I-II Maccabees concerns the control exerted over Judaea by the Seleucid dynasty, particularly Antiochus IV Epiphanes (215-164BC) [fig. 4]. I Maccabees covers the period from 175-134BC while II Maccabees focusses on the period of 180-161BC. Many of the events noted in these two books appear to be historical, and are corroborated in Josephus' *Antiquities*, which was written in the 1st century AD. I-II Maccabees follow the history of Mattathias of Modiin [fig. 5] and his four sons, amongst whom was Judas, known as 'Maccabeus'. While I Maccabees recounts the development of the Hasmonean kingdom from its earliest beginnings, II Maccabees focusses on the character of Judas Maccabeus himself. Coin production by a Jewish dynasty only began in the 2nd century BC. The first to produce coins was John Hyrcanus I, of the Hasmonean dynasty which was established by his uncle, Judas Maccabeus [fig. 6] following a revolt from the Seleucid overlords. The collective 'Maccabees' came to describe the whole family and also the

Fig. 4

Fig. 5

18

Hasmonean dynasty which followed, but originally the term only applied to Judas and sometimes his brothers. It has been suggested that the name comes either from the Aramaic word 'makkaba', or hammer, in reference to the swift, hard battle tactics of the brothers or it could also come from the Hebrew initials of the battle-cry of the brothers:

Who among the gods is like you, Lord? (Exodus 15:11)

Deuicto exercitu Antiochi gratijsq. Deo actis, Iudas cum exercitu suo ad sanctorum mundationem et restaurationem conuertuntur, exciso altari holocaustorū prophanato.
Mahab: 1. Cap: 4.

4

Fig. 6

19

The struggle against Seleucid rule continued throughout Judas Maccabeus' lifetime and after his death the fight was carried on by his brothers Jonathan and then Simon. Provoked by the harsh measures enacted against Jewish religious practice by Antiochus IV, the brothers fought a bitter war until the capture of Jerusalem in 165BC. They cleansed the Temple, which had been defiled by pagan practices instituted by Antiochus and the re-dedication of the Temple is still commemorated today as the important Jewish festival of Hannukah. This celebrates the miracle of discovering an undefiled jug of oil for the menorah in the Temple, which although containing only enough oil for one day, lasted eight days until more oil could be procured. Antiochus' death in 164BC brought hostilities to a close temporarily and the subsequent dynastic struggles of the mid-2nd century BC meant that the Maccabees could sometimes support one rival Seleucid against another. Judaea remained turbulent however: Judas Maccabaeus fell in battle in 160BC, Jonathan was assassinated in 142BC by Diodotus Tryphon [fig. 7], a Seleucid usurper, and Simon was murdered by his own son-in-law in 135BC.

Fig. 7

The Hasmonean Dynasty

Simon had finally been recognised as the military commander and high priest of the Jews in 140BC, and therefore can be seen as the founder of the Hasmonean ruling dynasty which followed. Though Antiochus IV had died in 164BC, his successors on the Seleucid throne continued to exert pressure on Judaea, which was still technically a Seleucid province. While Judaea gained autonomy in 140BC, it was only in 129BC, at the death of Antiochus VII Sidetes [fig. 8], that the province gained independence under John Hyrcanus[1]. Hyrcanus only has a brief mention in

I-II Maccabees. Though his father Simon was granted the right to mint coins by Antiochus VII, it was not until Hyrcanus came to power that coins were produced:

I permit you to mint your own coinage as money for your country. (I Maccabees 15:6)[3]

These coins, and those of the rest of the dynasty, were small copper alloy coins. Their low value and specific imagery suggest that they were intended mainly for local usage while larger payments would have been paid in foreign silver coins.

The Temple Tax, as we will see in chapter 4, would have been paid in shekels of Tyre, which began to be minted at around this period [fig. 9 and fig. 10]. Tyre had produced its own coins until it became part of the Seleucid kingdom. In 126/5 BC however it became free of Seleucid domination and began to produce coins autonomously. Exodus 30:11-16 and Mishnah *Shekalim* 2.4 note that the half-shekel payment was required annually of all Jewish males over the age of 20. Other payments to the Temple included contributions for the fulfilment of vows, purchasing sacrificial offerings and the redemption price for the first born. Exactly when an annual tribute payment became standard is unclear. It probably became fully established at the time of the Maccabees/Hasmonean dynasty although such an annual

Fig. 8

Fig. 9

Fig. 10

tax may have been established earlier amongst diaspora Jews on the model of sending tribute to mother cities of colonies in the Phoenician and Greek world. The imagery on these coins (the Tyrian god, Melkart) was not problematic for use in Jewish religious practice as is sometimes thought since, as the Mishnah later describes (*Kelim* 12.7), valid coins cannot be defiled unless they are used as jewellery or weights and therefore the imagery on the coins is not relevant in cleanliness laws. The only thing that mattered was the value and purity of the coin. One curious fact about the Temple tribute was that though the payment was a half-shekel per male over 20, an additional payment had to be made to pay the money-changer's fee at the Temple. Most people would arrive at the Temple with other coinages which had to be changed into the required Tyrian shekels. So, in reality the tribute was a half-shekel plus the fee, the kolbon (or kalbon), which was 11 prutot. The Talmud even states the opinion that even if a person went to the Temple with the exact half-shekel of Tyre in hand, he would still have to pay the surcharge to sanctify the payment since as it was made by humans it was not perfect. This is true in a very specific way – the half-shekel could not have been pure silver and so the payment of a surcharge would bring the payment up to the equivalent value of a pure half-shekel. The money changers who we will come to in the Gospels (chapter 4) set up their stalls across the country to collect the annual Tribute once a year, at the beginning of the month of Adar, preceding Passover, but were generally set up in the Temple courtyard year round.

The Hasmoneans were both kings and high priests of Jerusalem. The Herodian kings, who ruled afterwards, were not also high priests as they came from Idumenea and were therefore not eligible to be priests. According to Josephus (*Antiquities* 13.299), John Hyrcanus was:

considered by God to be worthy of the three privileges: the government of his nation, the office of the high priesthood, and prophecy.

John Hyrcanus' coins set the pattern for the rest of the Hasmonean dynasty [fig. 11]. The inscription on the obverse of the prutah reads 'Yehohanan the High Priest and the Council of the Jews' in proto-Hebrew script and the image on the reverse is a double cornucopia decorated with ribbons encircling a pomegranate. Hyrcanus' coins were therefore very different from those produced in neighbouring states. There, it was common for images of the ruler to appear on the obverse and a variety of gods or mythological figures on the reverse. In places, like

Tyre, where there was no king, the dominant image was of the local god, like Melkart, the Tyrian Heracles. Hasmonean coins however adhere to the strictures of the Second Commandment forbidding graven images. Hyrcanus' other coins also followed this rule, the half-prutah [fig. 12] has a lily for example[3a]. The double-prutah [fig. 13] however has a helmet on the reverse. This looks much more like the Greek coinages from surrounding areas, but the Hasmonean version has no head within the helmet thus complying with religious law.

Fig. 11

Fig. 12

John Hyrcanus was undoubtedly the greatest Hasmonean king. After his death in 104BC, his descendants ruled for a further sixty years or so but with less prestige and increasing Roman influence in their rule. Hyrcanus' son Judas Aristobulus I only reigned for one year or less, striking coins in the name of 'Yehudah the High Priest and the Council of the Jews' but otherwise in the same manner as his father [fig. 14]. Alexander Jannaeus (104-76BC), a younger son of Hyrcanus, was the first

Fig. 13

Fig. 14

Hasmonean ruler to adopt formally the title 'king'. His reign was long for a Hasmonean king, but was marked by almost continuous warfare. Jannaeus' continued contact with his Greek neighbours no doubt influenced his innovation of bilingual coin inscriptions – in proto-Hebrew and Greek. Jannaeus' first coins were similar to his brother's and father's coins [fig. 15], which name 'Yehonatan the High Priest and the Council of the Jews'. Jannaeus' other coins however, still observing the Second Commandment, have the dual inscription 'Yehonatan the King' in proto-Hebrew script and 'Alexander the King' in Greek [figs. 16 and 17].

Fig. 15

Following the death of Alexander Jannaeus, power probably passed to his queen, Salome Alexandra (Shlomozion) who appears to have ruled on behalf of her sons although she minted no coins. Her son John Hyrcanus II (Yonatan) was appointed high priest and therefore the heir to the throne but when Salome Alexandra died in 67BC, his younger brother, Aristobulus II challenged and overthrew him. Hyrcanus fled Jerusalem to the Nabataean king Aretas III and by conceding territory persuaded him to bring the Nabataean army to besiege Jersusalem in 65BC. Before his removal or after his restoration, John Hyrcanus II may have produced coins in the manner of his ancestors [fig. 18] with the inscription 'Yonatan the High Priest and the Council of the Jews' but it is not clear that these coins belong to him. This coin is from a series which appear to have been struck over the previous coins of Jannaeus. Hyrcanus' brother, Aristobulus II appears to have struck no coins at all, and

Fig. 16

Fig. 17

Fig. 18

Hyrcanus regained power in 63BC reigning until 40BC. The short reign of Mattatiyah Antigonus (40-37BC) was much more productive [fig. 19] and he followed the bilingual coinage of Judah Aristobulus with the proto-Hebrew script inscription 'Mattatiyah the High Priest and the Council of the Jews' on the obverse and 'of King Antigonus' in Greek on the reverse. His other coins also conformed to the prohibition on graven images but there is one innovation during Antigonus' reign which may have been controversial at the time. The 'Menorah' coin [fig. 20] is an important development in design and a significant image in Jewish religious life. Both the showbread table on the obverse and the menorah on the reverse have huge religious significance. The reasons for its production are unclear but it must surely have been to do with propaganda produced by the Hasmoneans in the last years before Herod I (the Great) defeated them and came to power. The status of the Hasmonean kings as high priests would have been contrasted with Herod's status as a potential king, but ineligibility to hold the position of high priest. The use of images explicitly stating a connection to the Temple and its rituals therefore signifies the Hasmonean position. The use of the menorah is unusual though not without contemporary examples on other items. The Babylonian Talmud, probably first written in the 3rd-5th centuries AD, forbids the reproduction of Temple items and contains a specific reference to the menorah and showbread table.

Fig. 19

Though the choice of images on Hasmonean coins may appear to have been restricted by the Second Commandment, they recall important design elements in Jewish tradition, which have later resonance in Christian art. Some of the images, particularly the cornucopia, had been popular in the eastern

Fig. 20

Mediterranean area for a number of years before appearing on Hasmonean coins. This use elsewhere may have influenced the choice of the image for the first Hasmonean coins. The imagery of the 'horn of plenty' was a widespread and popular representation of fertility and this may have found significance within Jewish culture with reference to Israel as a land of plenty and the horn symbol recalling the animal horns used as oil containers or as musical instruments ('shofars'). The use of the anchor on various Hasmonean coins may also have been influenced by its widespread use by the Seleucid dynasty, for so many years rulers over Judah. More specifically Jewish are the pomegranate and lily symbols. The pomegranate has a long history of decorating religious items, including in the Temple (according to Josephus *Antiquities* 8.3.4) and the robes of the high priest (Exodus 25-26). It was thought that the pomegranate had 613 seeds – the number of commandments in the Torah. The lily was also a symbol used on religious items and Josephus notes it as a decorative element in the Temple. It was considered a symbol of Jerusalem itself and a curious Seleucid coin struck in 132/131BC at the beginning of the reign of John Hyrcanus I may have been struck jointly with the Seleucid king Antiochus VII Sidetes at the beginning of the independent reign of the Hasmonean dynasty [fig. 21]. The use of the lily here in combination with the anchor brings both Jewish and Seleucid imagery together and it is generally assumed that this coin was struck in Jerusalem.

Fig. 21

Hasmonean coins, like most coins of this period, could have circulated for hundreds of years after their manufacture. Silver (and indeed gold) coins could circulate for a long period and geographically widely because of the intrinsic value of their precious metal. The lower value bronze coins took on a token value and generally did not circulate far from their point of origin. The worn state of the Hasmonean coins in many collections today point to their continued use as small change even after the end of the dynasty. The Gospel story of the Widow's Mite (Mark 12:42), as we shall see later, places great emphasis on the tiny coins used by the poor widow. This may well refer to the coins of Alexander Jannaeus, by far the most numerous small coins circulating in the area, rather than the contemporary small bronzes issued by the Roman governors at the time of the Gospels.

Chapter Three

THE HERODS (40 BC – AD 95), MONEY IN THE TIME OF JESUS

It should be surprising that the date of Jesus' birth remains a puzzle. After all, our dating system takes the start of the Common Era (or CE as AD is internationally known) from that event. Yet there is clearly a mistake in the medieval reckoning system of *Anno Domini* (in the year of the Lord). King Herod the Great died four years before the Common Era began. Thus, however strange it looks, 4 BC is where we are forced to place the last possible year for Herod's massacre of the innocents at Bethlehem in Judaea (Matthew 2:16), in his bid to eliminate the newly born rival King of the Jews. Furthermore, tax was not just a problematic issue later in the Jesus story, as we shall see, but it also proves awkward at the beginning. Herod I passed on a kingdom divided amongst his sons who could only officially call themselves by the sub-kingly title (which Herod I had briefly held himself during his rise to power) of 'ethnarch', ruler of a people, or 'tetrarch', ruler of fourth of a kingdom. (Although this is often ignored in Gospels and clearly the ordinary people were quite prepared to call the ethnarchs of these principalities by the title of king.) Judaea fell to the short-lived ethnarchy of Herod Archelaus, who was soon banished by the Romans in order to form a province of the empire in AD 6. This is the first possible year that a Roman tax census could logically have been conducted to establish a roll-call of taxpayers in the new imperial territory. If this was the tax census that took the soon-to-be-parents of Jesus to Bethlehem it leaves a serious chronological conundrum. Thankfully, dating the nativity story, with its prophesy-fulfilling birth connection to Judaea and specifically to King David's city of Bethlehem is beyond the purpose of this chapter looking at the coinages of Jesus's lifetime.[4] Nevertheless, it is convenient here to take it that the lifetime of Herod I just overlapped, and he is the king when Matthew (2:1) states Jesus was born "...during the time of King Herod".

Jesus grew up in Nazareth in Galilee, the area just to the north of Judaea, under the ethnarchy of another son of Herod I, Herod Antipas (4 BC-AD 39). His new capital city, Sepphoris was in much need of royal aggrandisement at this time (although his seat was later transferred to Tiberias on the sea of Galilee, a new foundation named after the emperor Tiberius). Bearing in mind Jesus's own family background in carpentry, such building work would have doubtless lured Nazarene craftsmen who were a walkable, distance away from Sepphoris itself. The central action of the Jesus story is the ministry (teaching) and the self-sacrificial act of the crucifixion. But when did this occur? The reign of the ethnarch Antipas is one fixed historical point. Another is the term of office of the fifth governor (prefect) of neighbouring Roman Judaea, Pontius Pilate, AD 26-36. Pilate's master was the second Roman emperor, Tiberius, AD 14-37. Alongside Pilate as joint protagonist representing officialdom in the trial and condemnation of Jesus was Joseph Caiaphas, the high priest of the Temple, during AD 18-36/7. Since the establishment of the Herodian dynasty, the high priesthood had been a separate office from king/ethnarch; Herod I had not been of priestly stock and was consequently debarred from the role along with his descendants.

We are told Jesus was 'about' thirty years old when his ministry began (Luke 3:23) and that this is marked by his baptism by John the Baptist. John's own ministry we are also told had begun:

In the fifteenth year of the reign of Tiberius Caesar [i.e. AD 28/9] – when Pontius Pilate was governor of Judea, Herod [Antipas] tetrarch of Galilee, his brother Philip tetrarch of Iturea and Traconitis, and Lysanias tetrarch of Abilene (Luke 3:1)

The terms of office of those in power – kings, tetrarchs, high priests and Roman governors – are luckily chronicled by the great first century Jewish historian Flavius Josephus (writer of *Jewish Antiquities* and the *Jewish War*), so we can be quite certain of their dates. While considering the activities of Pontius Pilate, Josephus does also mention in passing the execution of Jesus and the continuation of his following afterwards (*Antiquities* 18.63-4). Unfortunately the authenticity of the passage (also known as the *Testamonium Flavianum* – i.e. of Flavius Josephus) is severely limited by the later pious Christian interpolation modifying the copies which have come down to us.

The majority of Gospel accounts of the ministry of Jesus suggest it lasted one year, spanning one Passover (the annual springtime festival celebrating the Jewish Exodus from Egyptian slavery). Alternatively, it spanned at least three Passovers according to the Gospel of John (John 2:23, 4:45, 6:4, 11:55 etc), prior to Jesus's arrest, trial and crucifixion. A final snippet of chronological information helps fix the historical climax of Jesus's life to the years just prior to AD 30. We are told Jesus visited the Temple in the 46th year since its construction (John 2:20).

It may come as a surprise that the venerable Temple of Jerusalem should have been a new-build. Yet tearing down the old Temple and replacing it was one of Herod the Great's big building projects; construction lasted about eight years and was begun around AD 20/19 (*Antiquities* 15. 380; 421). Thus the visit of Jesus would have been around AD 26/27.[5]

The Temple rebuild could be seen as one outlet to make up for Herod's insecurity, a way of making his mark on a people and their faith of whom we get the distinct impression viewed him as an outsider. Not only was he of a non-priestly family (hence the need for a separate high priest – see chapter 2), but he was the grandson of a Jewish convert, from Idumaea, the land of Edom to the south of Judaea proper. The circumstances of Herod's rise to power could hardly have set him in good favour with the Jewish people. The son of a senior court official at Jerusalem, he managed to ingratiate himself with Mark Antony late in the 40s BC. Sweeping to power with Roman military might, he deposed the last priest-king of the Hasmonean dynasty in 37 BC and married his daughter, Mariamne, no doubt to bolster his position. The Jewish people's feelings at such foreign-imposed regime change was reciprocated by Herod with the sort of behaviour typical of tyranny; both the Bible and the secular writings of Josephus record a reign of notable harshness. Perceived political threats were met with swift execution and this included close family members. Mariamne and her sons were among those executed thus extinguishing the direct Hasmonean line. This character of suspicion and retribution is the background to the Biblical story of the massacre of the innocents; a man capable of responding with lethal force to any threat to his position of King of the Jews, no matter how ill-perceived. It is a matter of conjecture how much this was noticed by or mattered to the first Roman emperor Augustus (31 BC – AD 14), himself no stranger to ruthlessness in politics.[6] But by then Herod had made friends with the new regime too, and was clearly a useful Roman ally as the longevity of his reign proved. Students of history will quickly note that monarchs acquire the epithet, 'the Great', through the magnificence of their reign, seldom through the content of their character. Not only was Herod's territory greater than that (individually) of his sons but it included a number of notable new building works besides the Temple. The new coastal city of Caesarea Maritima ('Caesarea on Sea'– named after Caesar Augustus) was begun, symbolic of the new regime's Mediterranean orientation towards the Roman Empire. It had one of the largest man-made harbours of the ancient world and this new adornment to the kingdom made the traditional anchor device often seen on Jewish coinage a particularly appropriate symbol [fig. 1]. Caesarea would later become the seat of the Roman governors of Judaea. Herod's grip on his people was reinforced by a string of fortified hill-palaces. These included Herodium near Bethlehem which would become the king's burial place and further out, near the Dead Sea, that of Masada, scene of the last ditch resistance of the Zealots at the bitter end of the first Jewish Revolt (AD 73).

The imperial nature of Herod's regime and that of his successors is also reflected in the exclusively Greek legends of all Herodian coinage, the official language of the Roman east. Nevertheless, it does almost always respect the Jewish prohibition of graven images of animate objects; instead we have mostly the continuation of the kind of symbols which would not have seemed out of place on the coinage of the Hasmonean priest-kings. All the Herodian coinage consisted of bronze small change for use in local marketplaces; silver was imported and is discussed separately in chapters 2 and 4.

Fig. 1

Given the diminished spiritual role he played in relation to his predecessors, there is one coin type of Herod that is particularly suggestive of his emphasis of kingly authority. [fig. 2] This small bronze shows a reverse of a three-legged table, probably bearing some liturgical vessel, but the front of the coin, carrying the legend of the issuing authority (King Herod), depicts a diadem, the traditional headband symbol of royalty since the time of the Persian and Hellenistic empires. Within is a cross. This has occasionally drawn spurious claims to Christian influence in later ages but this pre-Christian coin type does help to explain Jesus' messianic name, Christ, in terms of Jewish kingship. Although it is similar to some forms of the Hebrew letter tav which was marked on the forehead in Ezekiel 9:4, the cross is probably an X, or Greek letter chi. According to the compendium of Rabbinical traditions known as the Talmud, priests anointed the King of the Jews by drawing a diadem ('circle round the head') and the letter chi (Talmud, *Kerithoth* 5b).[7] Chi is also the first letter of XPICTOC (Christos), which means the anointed. The

Fig. 2

cross gesture to the forehead had been noted as Christian ritual from as early as the second century AD (Tertullian *de Corona* 3.25-30).

Another coin type also inadvertently heralds the Christians with the inclusion of a tau-rho monogram (combining the Greek letters 'T' and R = 'P') which will be discussed in a Christian context later [fig. 3] Its significance is unclear. Parallels with other Roman period provincial coinage suggest it could stand for tetrarch (ΤΕΤΡΑΡΧΟΣ), the title Herod held in the few years after his alliance with Antony (begun 42 BC) but prior to taking full kingship with his victory of 37 BC. Using the demotic symbol for year (resembling the letter L) the coin denotes it was produced in regnal year three, LΓ (Greek letter gamma). The third year of Herod's appointment as tetrarch was 40/39 BC – a time of military strife for which the helmet design on the reverse would be most appropriate. But this would render Herod's title of full king (ΒΑΣΙΛΕΩΣ) in the legend puzzling.[8]

Fig. 3

The exception to the otherwise appropriately Jewish character of Herod's coinage can be seen in the eagle type [fig. 4], an undeniably graven image. It could be a Roman eagle or simply represent kingship generally (e.g. the eagle had been the totemic symbol of the Ptolemies of Egypt; Herod had been a contemporary of the famous Cleopatra VII, the last of that dynasty). However, when Herod tried to have a golden eagle affixed to the Temple gate it was promptly torn down by the faithful in a fit of religious outrage. True to character, Herod responded with execution of the perpetrators who were burnt to death (*Antiquities* 17.151-167).

Fig. 4

The major difference between the coinage of Herod I and that of his son and brief successor at Jerusalem, Herod Archelaus was the latter's use of the explicit title of ethnarch [fig. 5]. When Archelaus was banished to the other side of the empire in 6 AD, the mint at Jerusalem continued to produce similar small copper coins under the Roman governors. The coins were now in the name of the emperor only. However, they were handily dated with the emperor's regnal year. Thus we know that a specimen bearing the date 'LIZ', using the demotic symbol for year (L) and the Geek number 17 (17th year of Tiberius) was made AD 30-1, around the time of the climax of the Jesus story – and under the authority of the then governor Pontius Pilate. [fig. 6]

We know such humble coins were generically called *lepta* (sing. *lepton*) in Greek and in the next chapter we will consider just how low the smallest of these were. They were produced in a suite of denominations and it seems likely that there was the equivalent of the Roman as (shown in the next chapter), (e.g. of a full denomination unit = Fig. 3) together with fractions of a half, a quarter (e.g. Fig. 2), and an eighth. An eighth, seemingly the *prutah* of old, was below any denomination regularly used at Rome with important implications in its Biblical usage, as we will see. The other coins of this chapter so far possibly represent *prutot*

Fig. 5

Fig. 6

[figs. 4-6], but with fig. 4 possibly an even smaller half-*prutah*.[9] It is worth emphasising that such denominational judgements are often highly subjective since such ancient pieces lack the explicit indications of value of modern coins.

With the coinage of Herod Antipas (4 BC – AD 39) we can see the sort of small change produced for the everyday marketplaces of early first century Galilee. No doubt the prutot produced

Coin denominations of Galilee under Antipas

Units	Figs. 7a-d
double	
unit	
half	
quarter	

at Jerusalem would have been most acceptable too, but Antipas's mint otherwise appears to have avoided production of the smallest coins. Instead the suite of Galilean denominations probably ran from a double unit down to a unit, a half, and a quarter.[10] The designs were very similar across the denominations, proclaiming Antipas with the title of tetrarch [figs. 7a-7d].

Missing so far from this discussion of Herodian coinage is any images of the royal family themselves, but they do exist. The main obstacle to portraiture was Jewish religious sensibility but another one of Herod's sons, Herod Philip inherited the non-Jewish part of the kingdom. As tetrarch of Gaulanitis, Trachonitis, Batanea, and Paneas he had more freedom to produce portrait coinage [fig. 8] although it is rare in comparison to his non-portrait types. Although Philip is not particularly relevant to the Biblical story, his wife Salome certainly was; the alluring princess who demanded John the Baptist's head in return for a saucy dance for her step-father Antipas (Mark 6:22-5). It is sometimes thought that she is depicted on a coin of Armenia

Fig. 8

Minor in a subsequent marriage (Philip died in AD 34) to King Aristobulus (AD 54-92) but this is usually considered a later generation of Jewish princess.[11] For Aristobulus was himself the son of Herod, king of Chalcis (AD 41-8), who together with his brother Herod Agrippa I, as grandchildren of Herod the Great represent the next generation of Herodians. One of Herod of Chalcis's coins shows a possibly slightly presumptive view of their relationship with Rome, for the brothers stand, crowning the emperor Claudius.[fig. 9] Agrippa I (AD 37-44), had managed to win the most favour and seems to have become a close personal friend of the emperor, for

Fig. 9

Rome allowed him to inherit all his grandfather's kingdom. Even the Roman province of Judaea was briefly relinquished allowing him to become the first King of the Jews since Herod the Great with direct control over the Jewish heartlands, although this was denied to his son Agrippa II who we will consider later in the context of the Jewish revolts. Agrippa I's lower coin denominations carried on the format of his predecessors, including an interesting type with canopy or parasol to shade the ruler from the sun when in the public outdoors, a very traditional symbol of Middle Eastern kingship. [fig. 10] However, Agrippa I also became the first King of the Jews to have his effigy on a coin, along with a representation of his son [fig. 11] – all religious sentiments were now clearly sidelined. With Herod Agrippa we have now reached the AD 40s; after the time of Jesus, and firmly into the next chapter of the Christian story; the time of the ministry of St Paul, whose letters (epistles) form the earliest written parts of the New Testament.

Fig. 10

Fig. 11

Chapter Four

MONEY AND THE GOSPELS

Matthew, Mark, Luke and John. The order of the Gospels trips off the tongue for those with even a passing familiarity with the Bible.[12] The first three bear some close similarities in their narratives and are grouped together as the 'synoptic' gospels. It was only during the last century that textual comparisons between the synoptics began to suggest to Biblical scholars a specific chronological order. Rather than being an abridged version of Matthew, the brief gospel of Mark probably represents the first narrative of the story of Jesus Christ that has come down to us. Furthermore, there are various clues in the text – including references to coins – that suggest the work seems to be speaking to those in the heartlands of the Roman Empire and explaining things to those foreign to the first century Levant. Although the nature of the subject makes complete consensus impossible, Biblical scholars accepting this *Markian priority* could entertain the possibility that Mark was written somewhere to the west of the Levant (for example there was a growing Christian community at Rome itself) around AD 70.[13]

This would make the other synoptics, Matthew, and Luke, later narratives. These writers had access to Mark and possibly another written down source of the sayings of Jesus from which to draw common additions to the story. This hypothetical source (usually called 'Q' after the German for

41

fig. 1, Jericho road

source, 'quelle') would have taken the form of a simple list of quotations. This is certainly not as far-fetched as it sounds since the non-canonical (i.e. not in our modern Bible) gospel of Thomas came to light on ancient papyri in Egypt in 1945.[14] Although Thomas is not accepted as Q itself, it does take the expected format – simply a list of sayings without a narrative. For the faithful, one tradition identifies Mark as St Peter's interpreter (Eusebius, *Ecclesiastical History*, 3.39.14-16) and Mark's source could simply have been direct oral tradition, gleaned prior to Peter's martyrdom at Rome in Nero's persecutions in the AD 60s.

In addition to writing the longest and most detailed Gospel, Luke also wrote a sequel to the Jesus story, the Acts of the Apostles, chronicling the subsequent missionary work carried on by the Apostles). In any case, the chronology of the creation of the New Testament as it is most commonly recognised nowadays is first the letters of St Paul written during his mission to evangelise the Gentiles (non-Jews) in the Roman Empire in the 30s–50s AD. This is followed by Mark, AD 70s, and the rest of the New Testament in the subsequent decades. The final book of the New Testament is also its most mysterious; the apocalyptic visions detailed in the Book of Revelation are also generally thought to postdate Mark.

The language used by most of the characters in the Gospels would have been Aramaic, the local language which had long replaced Hebrew by Jesus's time. Yet the New Testament was written in Greek. More specifically, New Testament Greek was known as Koine, a simplified and internationalised version of the language of Sophocles and Plato. It was the perfect language for the proselytising missionaries of the New Testament who, ever since St Paul, had turned their attention to the people beyond the Aramaic-speaking areas. Koine was the 'Globish' (global English) of the Roman Empire. It could be understood by officialdom and by civilians alike at Jerusalem and even at Rome, which by this time had a significant population originating from the Hellenised areas of the eastern Mediterranean. It was therefore as natural for Paul to write his letters to the Romans in Greek as it was for him to do likewise for the other Christian communities in Greek cities of Corinth or Philippi. Paul could even confront Greek-speakers in person, most notably at Ephesus in the AD 50s. The magnificent city was the centre of one of the greatest pagan cults of the Greek world and the scene of the clash in the great theatre between the Christian missionary and the devotees of Artemis.

But when they realized he was a Jew, they all shouted in unison for about two hours: "Great is Artemis of the Ephesians!" (Acts 19:34) *[figs. 2a & 2b]*

Coin denominations at Rome c.AD 70 [figs. 3a-f]
The Christian communities at Rome around AD 70 would have been familiar in their financial transactions with a suite of coin denominations made of gold, silver and base metal. The highest was the gold aureus, a coin roughly 18-

Fig. 2a

20mm in diameter worth 1,600 times the lowest denomination, the quadrans. The quadrans was of similar size but lacked the emperor's bust and was made of copper and thus less than half the weight of a 7½g aureus. Also of similar size but different metal was the silver denarius, worth 1/25th of its gold counterpart. Below the denarius was a range of base metal coins including the copper as (assarion in New Testament Greek), at four times the quadrans its value was suggested by its larger size and weight, typically 8-10g. The double as was known as the dupondius and although it was of similar size in terms of circumference to its half denomination (but often thicker and heavier); its greater value was signalled by its brassy alloy known as orichalcum (reckoned by the Romans to be worth twice copper[15]). The dupondius also often used a radiate image (the emperor's head wearing a diadem emanating the sun's rays instead of a laureate or wreathed head). The sestertius was a double dupondius, also made of brass but

Fig. 2b: The great theatre at Ephesus today with view towards harbour.

Units	Figs. 3a-f	
aureus		
denarius		
sestertius		
dupondius		
as		
quadrans		

much wider, thicker and consequently heavier (over 24g compared to the dupondius average of 12-14g). The denarius, sestertius, and the as could all be used as units of account in Roman documents specifying sums of money, although the sestertius was more familiar as a unit in the west than the east.[16]

Small change in the Gospels, from the widows 'mite' and upwards
To an inhabitant of Rome, the quadrans (*kodrans* in Greek, a language widely spoken in Rome too) was the lowliest coin. Its lack of value was proverbial. The Roman readers of the Satyricon (Petronius's late first century AD satire on the social mores of the times set in Italy) would have understood, and been amused by, the description of a truly mean or grasping individual: someone who was 'ready to pick a quadrans out of the dung-heap (*stercore*) with his teeth' (*Satyricon*, 33.43).

Mark had a dilemma; he needed to explain to the occidental reader that the Levantine provincials had an even lower coin, (known colloquially as a 'mite' in English translations of the Bible). The incident occurs during the collection of offerings for the Temple:

Many rich people threw in large amounts. But a poor widow came and put in two lepta, worth a quadrans (ΛΕΠΤΑ ΔΥΟ Ο ΕCΤΙ ΚΟΔΡΑΝ). Calling his disciples to him Jesus said, "I tell you the truth, this poor widow has put more into the treasury than all the others. They all gave out of their wealth; but she, out of her poverty, put in everything – all she had to live on." (Mark 12:42-4)

Jesus is explaining that those with less to spare are making a bigger financial sacrifice. The metaphor is made by emphasising the relative face value of a coin, the most humble denomination of the small change encountered in the Levantine streets in the first century. This local small change was different in appearance but not unrelated to the official Roman coinage. The evangelist Mark's problem was that his readership's evident familiarity was only with coins stretching down to a quadrans or quarter of an as but clearly in the story there was something of even lower value. In much the same way an accessible piece of modern text might inform a British reader that a euro- or a US-cent is worth less than a British penny. In contrast, if we move beyond Italy and the western Mediterranean, an inhabitant of late first century AD Roman Britain would be unfamiliar with anything smaller than an as. We know from archaeology that quadrantes produced at Rome did not find their way to the island in any significant quantity.[17]

Mark's solution to the Roman Empire's differing zones of small change circulation was to elaborate that the two small coppers, *two lepta,* were *worth a quadrans*. It is worth noting that this tradition of adapting the Biblical narrative for the audience has long continued. In the first printed modern English translation of the New Testament in 1525, William Tyndale had to make his own colloquial adaptation to make sense in Renaissance England. Although translating direct from the Greek, he may well have been taking in mind *minuta,* a later Latin translation of Mark's Greek *lepta.* Nevertheless, Tyndale was essentially borrowing the notion of an equally minute coin from a neighbouring land, one in which he had languished while exiled from his persecutors; the Flemish *mijt.* This tiny copper coin was much smaller than anything circulating in Henry VIII's England which relied principally on silver coinage down to a ¼ fraction (farthing) of a standard silver penny. By contrast the Low Countries had a circulation that had in the *mijt* a coin worth 1/32 of their standard silver piece or *stuiver.* [Figs. 4 & 5] In the Tyndale Bible we are told "...And ther cam a certayne povre widowe and she threwe in two mytes which make a farthynge." Thus the story is fixed in English as the parable of the "widow's mites".

Figs. 4 & 5: double mijt & Henry VIII farthing

48

The smallest of small change also makes an appearance in Luke 12:57-59 in considering the fate of an imprisoned debtor:

I tell you, you will not get out until you have paid the last lepton (ECXATON ΛΕΠΤΟΝ).

In modern parlance from English translations of the Bible we would talk of a debt being paid to the last penny but here it is not necessary to stipulate a face value, the reader of Luke just needs to think of the tiniest copper they know. In relating the same story, Matthew (5:26) opts more specifically for the more universal quadrans (ΚΟΔΡΑΝΤΗΝ – certainly understood the west and probably in much of the east too) rather than the generic Greek term for small copper, lepton.

There is one other case of the use of small change in the Gospels. Matthew 10:29 notes the cost of sparrows (as a foodstuff).

Are not two sparrows sold for an assarion (ACCAPIOY)?

Luke (12:6-7) opts for a bulk discount in relating the same lesson.[18]

Are not five sparrows sold for two assaria (ACCAPIΩN ΔYO)? Yet not one of them is forgotten by God. Indeed, the very hairs of your head are all numbered. Don't be afraid; you are worth more than many sparrows.

Tribute pennies – silver coinage used to illustrate obligation and wealth

The problem of interpretation also applies to serious money. Invariably this means silver in the Gospel stories; gold seems to hardly figure in everyday usage (with one exception, see Matthew 10, 9 below). The importance of silver is highlighted in the Gospel passage that is often quoted shorthand as "render unto Caesar..."

They came to him and said... Is it right to pay the imperial tax to Caesar or not? Should we pay or shouldn't we?" But Jesus knew their hypocrisy. "Why are you trying to trap me?" he asked. "Bring me a denarius (ΔHNAPION) and let me look at it." They brought the coin, and he asked them, "Whose image is this? And whose inscription?" "Caesar's," they replied. Then Jesus said to them, "Give to Caesar what is Caesar's and to God what is God's." And they were amazed at him. (Mark 12:14-17)

Furthermore, Matthew (22:19) explains why a denarius was requested:

"Show me the coin used for paying the tax." They brought him a denarius (ΔHNAPION)...

Roman readers would have recognised that the denarius was the type of coin needed to pay tax, it was the serious money used in the Roman state's revenue and expenditure. This passage has become known (through the King James translation) as the 'tribute penny', taking in the Roman name *tributum* for direct taxation but with the coin denomination translated for cultural relevance.

Taking the term denarius at face value, a denarius of c.AD 30 is often used to illustrate the 'tribute penny' [fig. 6]. Although it is not impossible that Jesus could have handled such a coin, it is unlikely, for the Levant had its own local supplies of silver coinage and early first century denarii from the Roman west are very rare as finds in the area.[19]

Fig. 6

Instead archaeological evidence points to the Levantine circulation of silver prior to the fall of the Temple (AD 70) originating overwhelmingly from Syria [fig. 7; Syrian tetradrachm].[20] In the Greek-speaking East, the term drachma was the equivalent of the Latin denarius and modern textbooks would identify fig. 8 with its Greek legends as a drachma. Moreover, Syria, the nearest neighbour

Fig. 7

of the Holy Land, preferred to mint its drachmae in multiples of four, known as a *tetradrachm*. Whether Jesus had held a drachm or a tetradrachm, Mark (followed in this instance by Matthew) would doubtless have found it easier to explain this to his readers simply as a denarius, there being no such silver multiple in common use in the west.

The value of a silver denarius-drachma to the man or woman in the Levantine street was understood.

Fig. 8

Or suppose a woman has ten drachmae and loses one (ΔΡΑΧΜΑΣ ΕΧΟΥΣΑ ΔΕΚΑ ΕΑΝ ΑΠΟΛΕΣΗ ΔΡΑΧΜΗ). Doesn't she light a lamp, sweep the house and search carefully until she finds it? (Luke 15:8)

Just what such a sum represented in terms of personal wealth is outlined in the parable of the labourers in the vineyard.

"For the kingdom of heaven is like a landowner who went out early in the morning to hire workers for his vineyard. He agreed to pay them a denarius for the day and sent them into his vineyard. About the third hour [i.e. of daylight divided into twelve hours whose length varied according to the time of year] *he went out and saw others standing in the marketplace doing nothing. He told them, 'You also go and work in my vineyard, and I will pay you whatever is right.' So they went. He went out again about the sixth hour and ninth hour and did the same thing. About the eleventh hour he went out and found still others standing around. He asked them, 'Why have you been standing here all day long doing nothing?' 'Because no one has hired us,' they answered. He said to them, 'You also go and work in my vineyard.' "When evening came, the owner of the vineyard said to his foreman, 'Call the workers and pay them their wages, beginning with the last ones hired and going on to the first.' The workers who were hired about the eleventh hour came and each received a denarius. So when those came who were hired first, they expected to receive more. But each one of them also received a denarius. When they received it, they began to grumble against the landowner. 'These who were hired last worked only one hour,' they said, 'and you have made them equal to us who have borne the burden of the work and the heat of the day.' But he answered one of them, 'I am not being unfair to you, friend. Didn't you agree to work for a denarius (ΔΗΝΑΡΙΟΥ)? Take your pay and go. I want to give the one who was hired last the same as I gave you. Don't I have the*

right to do what I want with my own money? Or are you envious because I am generous?' So the last will be first, and the first will be last." (Matthew 20:1-16)

It is worth quoting this passage in full as it makes clear that the denarius-drachma was considered a fair day's wage for a fair day's work in the most common line of work in pre-industrial societies, agricultural labouring. It was a sum probably physically paid out in base metal small change since we have already seen that a single denarius piece was an unusual coin in the east of the Roman Empire. (It was common enough to be paid in base metal: changing up when needed to the [precious metal] 'coin of the tax' kept the moneychangers in business.) Of course, just like the 'Tax Penny' was a term that made sense to the Jacobean readers of the King James version, Mark could have originally translated the coinage into a sum understandable to a western audience in the AD 70s. In any case, we can be confident that for first-century labourers in the Roman Empire, receiving the equivalent day rate of a full denarius was reasonable for a full day's work. Not to have "borne the burden of the work and the heat of the day" was simply unfair on those that did.

It is worth noting by comparison that the annual salary of the basic grade of Roman legionary at this period was 225 denarii, issued in thrice yearly stipends or payments (i.e. of 75 denarii).[21] The Latin stipendium equated to the term opsonion in Greek.[22] This certainly did not place a soldier at a disadvantage to a labourer since the agricultural cycle would only have provided the opportunity to sell day-labour for a small part of the year.[23]

Then some soldiers asked him, "And what should we do?" He replied, "Don't extort money and don't accuse people falsely—be content with your pay [ΟΨΩΝΙΟΙC = stipend]." (Luke 3:14)

The parable of the Good Samaritan informs us of the buying power of silver.

... Jesus said: "A man was going down from Jerusalem to Jericho, when he fell into the hands of robbers. They stripped him of his clothes, beat him and went away, leaving him half dead. A priest happened to

be going down the same road, and when he saw the man, he passed by on the other side. So too, a Levite, when he came to the place and saw him, passed by on the other side. But a Samaritan, as he travelled, came where the man was; and when he saw him, he took pity on him. He went to him and bandaged his wounds, pouring on oil and wine. Then he put the man on his own donkey, brought him to an inn and took care of him. The next day he took out two denarii (ΔΥΟ ΔΗΝΑΡΙΑ) and gave them to the innkeeper. 'Look after him,' he said, 'and when I return, I will reimburse you for any extra expense you may have.' (Luke 10:30-35)

Jerusalem and Jericho are less than twenty miles apart so it is a full day's walk or donkey amble. Depending on how long the Samaritan might spend in business at his destination (to avoid dangerous night-time travel one would set off first thing in the morning) it is clear that two silver coins were expected to realistically pay for a man's bed and board for at least three days (fig 4.01).[24]

Other New Testament passages use denarii-drachmae sums in ways that make it clear the reader is to marvel at the expenditure. In the story of Jesus anointed at Bethany we hear:

...a woman came with an alabaster jar of very expensive perfume, made of pure nard. She broke the jar and poured the perfume on his head. Some of those present were saying indignantly to one another, "Why this waste of perfume? It could have been sold for more than 300 denarii (ΔΗΝΑΡΙΩΝ ΤΡΙΑΚΟCΙΩΝ) and the money given to the poor." (Mark 14:3-5)

In other words the perfume was worth a sum of money equivalent to four military stipends (of 75 denarii) and thus well over a year's salary of one of the better off members of everyday society. (However, 300 denarii is a suspiciously round number and it is worth noting that in AD 84 – quite close to the time Biblical scholars think Mark's narrative was written down – there was a general military pay increase to 300 denarii a year.[25]) Also using the yardstick of a basic army salary of 225 denarii, in the feeding of the 5000 we learn the cost of such a communal meal would equal almost a year's pay for a Roman soldier:

> *By this time it was late in the day, so his disciples came to him. "This is a remote place," they said, "and it's already very late. Send the people away so that they can go to the surrounding countryside and villages and buy themselves something to eat." But he answered, "You give them something to eat." They said to him, "That would take more than two hundred denarii (ΔΗΝΑΡΙΩΝ ΔΙΑΚΟCΙΩΝ)! Are we to go and spend that much on bread and give it to them to eat?"* (Mark 6:35-37)

Other mentions of sums are perhaps harder for the modern reader to grasp. For example the famine price of wheat is given as a denarius per quart (Revelations 6, 6) and the Roman reader was clearly meant to understand this as extortionate. Books and scrolls were luxury objects in antiquity. Cost of the materials (papyrus or parchment) aside, a scribe might command the same amount of money for writing just 100 lines (in his best writing) as that of a whole day's wage for a labourer.[26] But with an incident of book burning we are confronted with a sum that represents an aristocratic level of wealth,[27] we are left floundering to understand the value.

> *A number who had practiced sorcery brought their scrolls together and burned them publicly. When they calculated the value of the scrolls, the total came to fifty thousand pieces of silver (ΑΡΓΥΡΙΟΥ).* (Acts 19:19)

Were there a lot of scrolls or were they particularly valuable because they were magic writings? In fact to confuse the issue further, the original report does not specify the denomination in question using the term pieces of silver; it is only modern Bible translation that translates specifically to drachmas (it could have been staters worth four drachmae-denarii apiece). The actual sum: five myriads of silver, ΑΡΓΥΡΙΟΥ ΜΥΡΙΑΔΑC ΠΕΝΤΕ, a myriad being a unit of 10,000)

It is perhaps best to return to the safer subject of taxation which started this section and look at the other institutional revenue and expenditure that faced first century Jewish society, the Temple.[28]

It is also a sly dig at the Roman state for which those in Italy lived tax free while provincials had to pay up:

After Jesus and his disciples arrived in Capernaum, the collectors of the two-drachma (ΔΙΔΡΑΧΜΑ) Temple tax came to Peter and asked, "Doesn't your teacher pay the Temple tax?" "Yes, he does," he replied. When Peter came into the house, Jesus was the first to speak. "What do you think, Simon?" he asked. "From whom do the kings of the earth collect duty and taxes—from their own children or from others?" "From others," Peter answered. "Then the children are exempt," Jesus said to him. "But so that we may not offend them, go to the lake and throw out your line. Take the first fish you catch; open its mouth and you will find a four-drachma piece (**CTATHPA** = stater). *Take it and give it to them for my tax and yours."* (Matthew 17:24-27)

It might at first be assumed that the Syrian tetradrachm was the most likely candidate for this incident. However, the temple required a special sort of silver coin, by dint of tradition. These were the tetradrachms and didrachms (4 and 2 drachmae pieces) of the city of Tyre, just to the north of the Holy Land [figs. 9 and 10 in chapter 2]. To use Semitic terminology these two silver denominations could also be known as a shekel and a half shekel. As mentioned in chapter 2, all payments to the Temple had to be made in 'Tyrian silver'. It seems at first unlikely that such pagan coin types featuring the head of the Semitic god Melkart-Heracles should be the preferred choice of the Jewish Temple, but they were the only silver coinage of the highest bullion purity readily available; another traditional requirement. Of the various standards of silver purity available in the eastern part of the empire in the first century only two were close to pure bullion: the 'Tyrian' standard and the 'Attic' (i.e. Athenian) standard most notably used for Roman denarii.[29] As already noted, Roman denarii were hard to come by in the Levant in the early part of the first century (with Syrian-made 4-drachmae coins of less pure silver being the usual substitute[30]) and the strength of the

Jewish tradition of Tyrian silver was clearly very strong. In fact it has been suggested from stylistic changes as well as archaeological findspot evidence that by the later first century BC production was transferred from Tyre to Jerusalem despite still carrying a Tyrian dating system. Although this latter view is not fully accepted, production died out during the year AD 65/6 – close enough to the eve of the first Jewish revolt to strongly suspect it was directly disrupted by the war.[31]

Thus it seems hopeful we can identify the most infamous sum of money mentioned in the New Testament, the thirty pieces of silver paid by the Temple authorities for the betrayal of Jesus.

Then one of the Twelve—the one called Judas Iscariot—went to the chief priests and asked, "What are you willing to give me if I hand him over to you?" So they counted out for him thirty pieces of silver (· Λ · ΑΡΓΥΡΙΑ). (Matthew 26:14-15)

Thirty shekels is a suspiciously proverbial sum repeated previously in scripture for compensation or wage payments (e.g. Exodus 21:32; Zechariah 11:12) and it might well have been a fittingly Biblical sum chosen by Matthew as a literary device. On the other hand it seems possible that the scripturally-aware temple authorities could have deliberately chosen a sum of thirty shekels to make a point. Also, even if the sum had not been exactly thirty shekels, at 120 denarii (possibly more depending on any exchange premium for such fine silver) the amount represented far more than a legionary's thrice annual stipend (75 denarii) and must have seemed a credible bribe to the ancient reader. Furthermore, some idea is given of the purchasing power of thirty such silver coins when we then hear that the tainted money was eventually put to a social use; purchasing land (the Potter's Field) to use as a foreigner's cemetery. This arose as a problem when Judas returned the payment. It had hitherto been acceptable silver for sacred purposes, but was now tainted:

So Judas threw the money into the Temple and left. Then he went away and hanged himself. The chief priests picked up the coins and said, "It is against the law to put this into the treasury, since it is blood money." So they decided to use the money to buy the potter's field as a burial place for foreigners. (Matthew 27:5-6)[32]

A bag representing the thirty pieces of silver, often with coins spilling out, is one of the Instruments of the Passion (the *Arma Christi*) and has been represented in art alongside the cross, sponge, spear of Longinus etc. (see chapter 7, fig. 17)

Moneychangers [fig. 9, detail of contorniate medallion showing a money changer's booth]

Had Judas kept the sacred silver, and his life, he would probably have needed to change it into everyday spending money. This business was traditionally conducted at booths set up prominently within the temple's forecourt. Money changers (nummularii) were not exclusive to Jerusalem. Travellers across the Roman Empire – officials, traders or pilgrims – would have to take a portable amount of money with them that might prove unsuitable for general use at their destination. Thus we hear Jesus give his followers counterintuitive advice for their journeying:

"Do not take along any gold or silver or copper in your belts" (Matthew 10:9)

We have already noted the need to change everyday money into Temple payments earlier in this chapter (and chapter 2). Another reason for the need to visit a moneychanger might be for a traveller to change down more valuable gold and silver coins (in which it is easier to transport large sums) into local small change suitable for everyday spending. The opposite service – changing up – meant moneychangers could furnish the local community with precious metal coins for taxation (for example the takings of small businesses were likely to have been in base metal small change suitable for small transactions); testing for forgeries as required. All this activity was conducted at a profit in

Fig. 9

57

whichever direction the coins were being changed. Investors could make a profit by supplying the nummularii with their working capital for a return on the business's profits. This is implied in the Parable of the Talents (very large sums of money expressed by weight of unspecified coins or ingots, or a mixture of both) which a lazy servant neglects to invest on behalf of his master:[33]

"His master replied, 'You wicked, lazy servant! So you knew that I harvest where I have not sown and gather where I have not scattered seed? Well then, you should have put my money on deposit with the bankers, so that when I returned I would have received it back with interest. (Matthew 25:26-27)

At Jerusalem, with its two different forms of taxation (secular and sacred), the Temple forecourt must have been particularly busy with commercial activity with traders calling out their wares (such as animals for Temple sacrifice) and moneychangers their exchange rates. This is the scene for the fateful event that sets Jesus on his collision course with the authorities; the cleansing of the Temple.

On reaching Jerusalem, Jesus entered the Temple courts and began driving out those who were buying and selling there. He overturned the tables of the money changers and the benches of those selling doves, and would not allow anyone to carry merchandise through the temple courts. And as he taught them, he said, "Is it not written: 'My house will be called a house of prayer for all nations'? But you have made it 'a den of robbers.'" (Mark 11:15-17)

Chapter Five

THE DOWNFALL OF JUDAEA (AD 66-135)

Fig. 1a sestertius of Titus Caesar illustrating the defeat of Judaea

As he was leaving the temple, one of his disciples said to him, "Look, Teacher! What massive stones! What magnificent buildings!" "Do you see all these great buildings?" replied Jesus. "Not one stone here will be left on another; every one will be thrown down." (Mark 13:1-2)

For Biblical scholarship, it is this passage foretelling the destruction of the Temple of Jerusalem that dates the writing of the Gospel of Mark to AD 70 or shortly after. In the summer of this year the climax of the First Jewish Revolt (AD 66-73) was played out in Jerusalem as the future emperor Titus at the head of three legions captured and sacked the temple, carrying off its holy treasures to

Fig. 1b

Rome. [fig. 1b] The war appears to have erupted from the long-term discontent of an occupied people but sparked by a local sectarian spat between the pagan and Jewish communities. It turned out to be a full scale war. Although the area of the revolt was contained within two years, prolonged sieges followed at Jerusalem, Gamla in the Golan and finally, the hilltop fortress of Masada. It was an expensive

Fig. 2

business for Rome and for a short time gold aurei were produced with Latin legends but in same engraving style as the local coins thought to have possibly been made at Caesarea Maritima, the administrative capital of Roman Judaea. These coins record Titus' IMPerator ('commander') title for successful military leadership acquired for the sack of Jerusalem on 6th August AD 70. [fig. 2] It is not too hard to imagine the obvious source of raw material for these local gold coins produced late in AD 70 or 71 in the aftermath of the sack: the Temple treasury itself. Indeed, that this largess was showered on the successful troops is implicit in one contemporary writer's statement on the obvious effect such an influx of gold had on the market.

… The sanctuary itself and all around it were in flames [the Romans] *carried their standards into the Temple court and…with rousing acclamations hailed Titus as imperator* [i.e. successful commander, a title carried on coinage]. *So glutted with plunder were the troops, one and all, that throughout Syria the standard of gold was depreciated to half its former value.* (*Jewish War* 6.316)

Incidentally, what that gold value should have been is specified in the same source in the course of a particularly grisly passage. Jewish refugees had taken advantage of the high value-to-weight portability that gold provided by swallowing aurei prior to their flight: *then escaping to the Romans, on discharging their bowels,* [they would] *have ample supplies to their needs* (*Jewish War* 6.421). Of course once in the refugee camps, the gold which had been bought so dearly from hastily liquidised assets became too plentiful and we are told that the normal value of an aureus set at 25 silver denarii became halved to twelve denarii (*Jewish War* 5.550: …δώδεκα γοῦν Ἀττικῶν… Josephus was writing in Greek, and used a common eastern terminology for denarius which was of the [good silver] 'Attic' [standard]). Worse still, once the camp guards spotted the gold being thus discharged, the refugees became targets for evisceration on the off-chance that they might be concealing such wealth: *actually in one night no less than two thousand were ripped up* (*Jewish War* 5.552)

The Romans had not been the only ones creating a war chest of money. The Judaean rebels produced their own coinage carrying dates referring to five years of the rebellion, AD 66-70 (the fifth year cut short by the fall of Jerusalem). Its Hebrew legends usefully stated their denomination on the front – together with the mint ('Jerusalem the holy') on the reverse [figs. 3a-c]. It was unusual for ancient coins actually to carry their denomination but clearly here the name was redolent with the sense of national identity such Hebrew coinage was at pains to impart: the shekel, together with half and quarter units. The most frequent designs were a holy vessel and a branch of pomegranates together with other objects used in Temple liturgy. The revolt coinage was intended to be a complete replacement at every denominational niche of what had been commonly circulating under Roman occupation and it even included bronze. [fig. 4] Small change being perhaps a surprising consideration during a desperate rebellion concerned with wartime expenditure.

With the fall of the Temple, its tax was now included as an addition to the state taxes, effectively a punitive tax on being Jewish. Remarkably, in the face of this calamity the Jewish king himself, Herod Agrippa II (AD c.49-c.95; he succeeded to his father's territories in stages) had been allowed to keep his throne. This feat had been achieved no doubt partly due to his lack of direct political control over Judaea (Agrippa II only had oversight of the religious affairs of the Temple of Jerusalem; his kingdom was actually confined to neighbouring lands). But also Agrippa II's unswerving loyalty to the emperor over his own

Units	Figs. 3a-c	
shekel		
half shekel		
quarter shekel		

Fig. 4

people must have played a part – his coinage only ever shows the discreet mention of the king's name on the reverse with the front given over to the emperor's portrait and titles [fig. 5]. (Agrippa II was destined to be the last Herodian king and gets a brief mention in Acts 26, 27-8 when Paul is brought before him prior to being deported to Rome for trial by the then governor of Judaea, Porcius Festus, around AD 59-60).

Although the Jewish tax itself was not abolished until the fourth century AD, soon after the downfall of Vespasian's son Domitian (AD 81-96) the corruption associated with this financial burden was in some part ameliorated, an event commemorated by his successor the emperor Nerva, AD 96-8. [fig. 6] The coin type employs the palm tree to represent Judaea and the legend FISCI IVDAICI CALVMNIA SVBLATA (the bringing of false / vexatious proceedings (*calumnia*) for the Jewish tax quashed (*sublata*)). Domitian's notably harsh rule had included harassment of those suspected of the Jewish tax evasion through disguising their faith. 'Outing' through intimate public examination could also inconvenience and humiliate the uncircumcised, according to the personal recollection of the writer Suetonius (*Twelve Caesars,* Domitian, 12). Christians too would have been counted by the Roman state as a Jewish sect and liable for taxation in this early period. The earliest male Christian followers followed the Jewish custom (and Jesus's example) of circumcision. However, within the lifetime of the apostles, a council of prominent Christians at Jerusalem (Acts 15) had consciously widened the appeal of the new faith to potential converts outside Judaism: circumcision was no longer compulsory. Perhaps

Fig. 5

Fig. 6

unsurprisingly in the face of Jewish hardships, this physically indelible mark of faith appears to have become swiftly abandoned in mainstream Christianity. Although it has never died out in some traditions such as the Coptic Church in Egypt and the Ethiopian Church, it was an early sign of the distancing of the two faiths which would develop over the course of the Jewish revolts of the first and second centuries AD.

Nerva's successor was Trajan (AD 98-117). The new emperor's father had commanded the tenth legion in Titus's army at the siege of Jerusalem; the son too found himself in conflict with the same people. A revolt of diaspora Jews in parts of North Africa, Cyprus and Babylonia occurred but the nadir was reached under Trajan's successor Hadrian (AD 117-38). He refounded Jerusalem, probably in AD 130[34] as the pagan Aelia Capitolina, dedicating the city both to himself through his family name Aelius and to Jupiter Capitolinus the high god of the Roman state (whose temple in the city was to be paid for by the Jewish tax). Hadrian also struck at the very heart of Jewish identity and banned circumcision (*SHA Hadrian* 14.2). [fig. 7a & b two coin types of Aelia Capitolina]

Fig. 7a

The second Jewish revolt followed in AD 132-5. Aelia-Jerusalem, now garrisoned by the tenth legion was never taken by the rebels who played out a long end-game with many holed up in the caves of the Judaean desert. The excavated cave remains has added a more hauntingly personal aspect to the Second Revolt and some of the names of the rebel protagonists from all social levels have come down to us. Firstly, unlike the First Revolt coinage, the Second Revolt coins carry the names of the leadership: 'Simon, prince of Israel' and 'Eleazar the priest'. Secondly,

Fig. 7b

the dusty final refuges of the rebels – most notably the 'Cave of Letters' (excavated in the mid-twentieth century) – have yielded a wealth of documents of the ordinary people caught up in the conflict.[35] There is even a letter from the leader himself revealing his full name, Simon Ben Kosiba. He had come down to us through history with the messianic surname Bar Kokhba ("Son of a Star" in Aramaic) and hence this final revolt of Judaea has also been known as the Bar Kokhba (or Kochba) war.

Fig. 8

The coinage of the Second Revolt was much more integrated with the locally available Roman coinage. In fact the Second Revolt coinage *was* the official coins overstruck (or reminted) with new designs. [fig. 8] In particular the silver drachm was much more commonly available by the second century, now

Fig. 9

joined in quantity by the western Roman denarius which had become plentiful in the region in the wake of the influx of legions during the first revolt. The second revolt documents tell us that the denarius-drachm was known in Aramaic as the *zuz*, and (pl.) *zuz'im*. Revolt coins have been found which clearly show their denarius undertype. [fig. 9] The tetradrachms (the 4-drachma piece known in Aramaic as *sela*) of Syria were also reminted by the rebellion. As one everyday financial document from the Cave of the Letters archive tells us:

> *Eleazar receives for the lease twelve silver zuzim which are three sela'im*[36]

The revolt sela provides us with an evocative image of the dashed hopes and aspirations of the Jewish people. [fig. 10] Its reverse slogan can be translated as 'the deliverance of Jerusalem' alongside a depiction of the ritual 'lulav' (a palm-branch tied together with willow and myrtle branches) and an etrog (citrus fruit). On the obverse (front) of this coin accompanying the name of Simon is a representation of the façade of the Temple at Jerusalem – destroyed since AD 70. It is represented in the typically abbreviated form seen on Roman coins representing pagan temples. These visual abbreviations were also keen to show the cult statue within as if it had somehow been moved out to the entrance to stand between the central columns. In the case of the Jewish Temple, the place of the cult statue is taken by the Ark of the Covenant (or possibly an Ark-like liturgical Shewbread Table; or even the temple door decoration).[37] Thus the image is a conflation of the recently lost second Temple combined with a reminder of the long lost treasure of the first Temple.

Fig. 10

Fig. 11:

ADVENTVI AVG IVDAEA coin

Simon ben Kosiba was unable to deliver Jerusalem or rebuild the Temple. In fact the war had quite the opposite effect, providing the Romans with the excuse to enact the *damnatio memoriae*, the final insult most often applied to banish the memory of disgraced emperors. During the governorship of Julius Severus (AD 133-5) who was called all the way from his previous post in Britain by Hadrian to finish off the revolt, the name of Judaea was obliterated and name of their Philistine (Palestine) neighbours now encompassed the whole land as 'Syria-Palaestina'.[38] Just prior to this 'Judaea' last appears on the coinage of Hadrian, part of a series commemorating the provinces. [fig. 11] As it shows a very Hellenic-looking province at sacrifice celebrating her pagan rebirth, the coin was made between the imperial visit of AD 130 and 133; the very eve of her destruction.[39]

The period of the Jewish wars (AD 66-135) had two major influences on the development of the Christianity. First there was a rebalancing of what had been the two main branches of the faith. The church of St James, which had taken root at Jerusalem itself, was obliterated in the First Revolt. It left the Pauline church which had taken root amongst the Gentiles evangelised by St Paul outside the Biblical lands, dominant. Secondly, it saw the growing Christian communities unsurprisingly trying to distance themselves from the financial and other hardships of the Jews. This is embodied by the correspondence of Pliny the Younger while governor of Bithynia and Pontus in Asia Minor (AD 110) to his master the emperor Trajan. Although he put many to death for their treacherous disrespect of the state religions (those Christians holding Roman citizenship he sent to Rome for trial, a situation that St Paul had faced half a century earlier), he was also the first Roman politician to consider their community in detail.

They had met regularly before dawn on a fixed day to chant verses alternately among themselves in honour of Christ as if to a god... (*Epistulae* 10.96.7)[40]

As the Christians left the shadow of Judaism, it was their propensity for organisation that was bringing their presence within the community to the notice of the authorities. That this and the unusually prominent acceptance of women within the faith were probable driving factors behind the growth is also revealed by Pliny.

This made me decide it was all the more the necessary to extract the truth by torture, from two slave-women, whom they call deaconesses. I found nothing but a degenerate cult carried to extravagant lengths. (*Epistulae* 10.96.8)

Chapter Six

Christian Dawn
(Roman Empire, 3rd Century AD)

There are few Christian artefacts until Christianity bursts into the open after the general toleration given by the Edict of Milan in AD 313. At Pompeii there are examples of a word game, the ROTAS-SATOR magic square (where the same words can be read in several directions) which might be Christian and certainly pre-date the AD 79 eruption of Vesuvius. These can be rearranged to spell out PATER NOSTER (our father, the beginning of the Lord's prayer) in the form of a cross (connecting at the N) with A and O left over (the significance of alpha and omega will be discussed below). The magic significance of words certainly chimes well with early Christian sensibilities as has already been discussed, but scholarship remains divided over whether ROTAS-SATOR squares can be considered exclusively Christian. Pompeii aside, the earliest securely dated Christian archaeological context comes from the house church at Dura-Europos, the doomed Roman city in the far east of Syria. The church (and nearby synagogue) found there must pre-date the destruction of the city by the Sassanid Persians in AD 256-7. [fig. 1]

There is remarkably one Old Testament Biblical scene depicted on coinage from the third century AD, during the last century of the pagan Roman Empire. It was minted at Apamea in Phrygia

Fig. 1 The House Church at Dura Europos (Eastern Syria)

(central Asia Minor) and depicts the story of Noah. [fig. 2] The coin reverse shows Noah and his wife twice. On the left they have arrived on Mt. Ararat but even more interestingly on the right they are in transit, adrift in the ark; shown, somewhat surprisingly to the modern viewer, as a simple box or rather a chest with lid (and conveniently labelled with Noah's name in Greek: NΩΕ). Above them the dove with olive branch sets the scene from Genesis 8:10-11:

Fig. 2

He waited seven more days and again sent out the dove from the ark. When the dove returned to him in the evening, there in its beak was a freshly plucked olive leaf! Then Noah knew that the water had receded from the earth.

An Old Testament subject would have been an unusual but uncontroversial reverse type in pagan Apamea. The reason for it remains unclear, for Mt Ararat lies on what is now the Turkish-Iranian border – hundreds of miles east the central Asia Minor lands of Phrygia. However, Apamea in Phrygia had a significant Jewish population from as early as the reign of the Seleucid king Antiochus III (222-187 BC) who resettled 2,000 Jewish families there from Babylonia. An old name for the city itself was Kibotos, Greek for 'chest' or 'coffer', possibly because of the significant position the city occupied in regional trade. Genesis 6:14 uses 'kibotos' to describe Noah's Ark and this may be another link to Apamea's use of the biblical story.[41] The 2nd – 3rd century AD was an age when subject cities of the Roman Empire might well select a geographical feature such as a mountain as a dramatic but politically neutral coin design to express their civic identity. But it should normally be a local mountain. One appropriate example is the view of Mt Gerizim on the coinage of the nearby town of Shechem (Neapolis in the Roman period) in Samaria. [fig. 3]

Fig. 3

Mt Gerizim was reportedly the site of an assembly of Israelites during the campaigns of Joshua (Joshua 8, 30-35). However, archaeological investigation of site has revealed that the temple shown on the coin type crowning the mountain, and reached by monumental staircase rising from a colonnade, to be dedicated to Zeus, king of the pagan gods. This was to be expected of given the staunchly pagan people of the area in Biblical times, hence the irony – from a Judeo-Christian viewpoint – of the helpful 'Good Samaritan' in Jesus' tale (see ch.4).

But what of artefacts associated with the oft-persecuted early Christians? New Testament subjects could obviously never appear as an official coin type before the fourth century. What sort of artefacts would we be looking for and how could we securely date it to the time of outlawed, underground sect? The mid-third century Dura-Europos house church contained paintings of Biblical subjects that stylistically follow the Jewish tradition from the nearby synagogue. Biblical texts survive from this period or perhaps even earlier, preserved in the dry heat of Egypt. However, a glance at any of these shows them to be from a book without pictures and in material culture terms early Christianity can be said to have lacked a distinctive repertoire in its visual language. But there is a way of turning a word into an emblematic symbol. If the letters are superimposed it is often possible to make a distinctive monogram. From the earliest Christian texts, there is a tendency to shorten sacred names (*nomina sacra*). For example, XPICTOC, the Greek word for Jesus's messianic name could be shortened to XP and thus Jesus Christ, IHCOC XPICTOC can appear as (IH XP) with a line over it (ligatured) to indicate its status. [fig. 4: Rev. 1:4-7 on London Pap 2053].

One reason for the practise of *nomina sacra* could have been to save precious space. After all books and scrolls were luxury products and a wordy book such as the Bible needed a lot of parchment or papyrus. The fourth century AD Codex Sinaiticus (from the monastery on Mt Sinai in Egypt), the earliest surviving complete Bible, has no illustrations and the text is crammed in without spaces

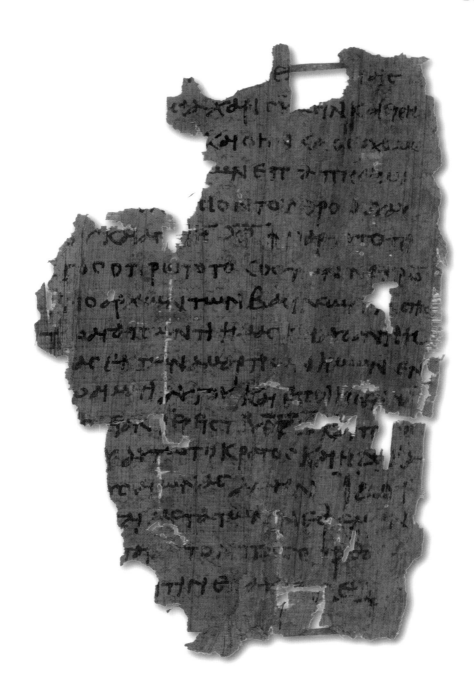

Fig. 4

between the words (*scriptio continua*). It contained an estimated 136,000-137,000 lines; and as already mentioned scribes were paid the equivalent of a basic day's wage for every 100 lines they completed in their best writing. 160 lines of such writing was the equivalent in material cost to a square foot of parchment. Codex Sinaiticus would have involved the slaughter of a herd of no less than 360 animals for their skins to create what would have originally ran to over a thousand huge pages (each approximately 40cm x 70 cm).[42] One estimate places the total fourth century cost of the Codex Sinaiticus at 19.7 contemporary gold pieces, just a little short of a priest's annual income at the time.[43] In fact there is a New Testament reference to the expense of books in the ancient world in the incident of the magic scrolls (Acts 19:19) mentioned in chapter 4.

On the other hand, it has also been noted that the amount of space saved by these select abbreviations is comparatively small and that the ligatured form of *nomina sacra* is similar to the convention indicating sums on ancient inscriptions (including coins).[44] Thus the origin of the practice might have been more influenced by the early Christian fascination with isopsephy; drawing numerological significance from words. In Greek and Latin counting systems numbers are simply expressed by letters (hence the need to distinguish sums with an overlining ligature). With isopsephy, phrases, words or their abbreviations viewed as numbers can take on good or ill-omened significance, while two words, such as a person's name and the quality with which they are associated, could have a special affinity when their letters add up to the same sum. An ill-omened example is the infamous 'number of the beast' in Revelation 13:18.[45] More prosaically a Christian might sign off a letter with '99', the sum total of the Greek numeral-letters in amen (AMHN).[46] A = 1; + M = 40; + H = 8; + N = 50. Incidentally, *nomina sacra* also made their way onto coins, but at a much later period and can be seen flanking the Byzantine bust of Jesus on Fig. 26 of chapter 7.

Another form of abbreviation is achieved by superimposing the first two letters, chi and rho to make a chi-rho monogram or Christogram. ☧ At the time of its adoption into a Christian context there was nothing new in the chi-rho monogram. Coinage demonstrates its use as early as the third century BC where it was in use as a mint official's mark at

Alexandria in Egypt.[47] [fig. 4] It is still found up to only a couple of generations prior to the fourth century edict tolerating Christianity issued at Milan, on local mid-third century AD coinage of Maeonia in Asia Minor as an abbreviation for the word archon, ΑΡΧΩΝ, the title of a chief civic magistrate. [fig. 6]

Fig. 5

Thus the British Museum's enigmatic graffito coin of Cyzicus in Asia Minor is one of the most beguiling Christian artefacts in its collection. [fig. 7] It is a very large bronze piece dating to the early third century AD. When it was struck bearing an imposingly brutal portrait of Caracalla (during his sole reign of AD 211-7), the empire was quite firmly and solidly pagan – the reverse shows the emperor addressing Hades, god of the underworld with the hellhound Cerberus at his feet. Two major persecutions of the Christians (AD 250s and the 'Great Persecution' of AD 303-11) lay between the period this coin was made and the AD 313 Edict of Milan. Furthermore this type of local bronze coinage would be swept away in major monetary reforms of the AD 290s, leaving the whole empire

Fig. 6

Fig. 7

supplied by a network of state branch mints producing a new single standard currency. It seems all the more remarkable that an ancient owner should have taken this coin with its pagan view of the afterlife and Christianise it with Biblical words. Firstly a chi-rho has been deeply scratched behind the imperial bust. Below this a C-like lunate sigma, standing for Saviour (Acts 4:12 asserts that 'Salvation is found in no one else' other than Jesus) while opposite the bust is the first and last letters of the Greek alphabet, alpha and omega; A ω (with the latter on its side). Revelation 1:8 states:

"I am the Alpha and the Omega," says the Lord God, "who is, and who was, and who is to come, the Almighty."

Finally there is the Latin word for peace, PAX, written retrograde (in mirror image) towards the edge below the bust. The concept of Jesus as prince of peace comes from an Old Testament passage.

For to us a child is born, to us a son is given, and the government will be on his shoulders. And he will be called Wonderful Counsellor, Mighty God, Everlasting Father, Prince of Peace. (Isaiah 9:6)

Thus the whole run of graffiti reads: 'Christ Saviour, the first and last, peace'. But could it represent a secret token of a Christian during their time of persecution? It certainly appears possible that it may have been "adapted for use as a secret pass or identification ticket for Christians soon after its issue *circa* AD 215"[48] We can offer one other scenario that sadly might likely place it in a later and openly Christian world.

Although it is an object made and used in the Greek speaking east (the coin's legends are in Greek) it carries a Latin word, pax. The catacombs of Rome have long been known to include coins and medallions among the markers stuck into the walls of the burial niches (loculi). These underground burial galleries grew out of the need to maximise space for the fashion for inhumation that began to replace cremation from the second century AD. Early hypogea (underground tombs) fully developed into the galleries of stacked loculi by the fourth century AD. Remarkably, since

Fig. 8

clusters of coins spanning the second to the fourth centuries AD have been found embedded in the same niche wall, those made in earlier, pagan centuries could be kept as heirlooms and placed as markers on fourth century catacomb burials.[49] Surprisingly, given their western location, among them were the larger provincial coins made in Asia Minor and the Levant.[50] Indeed, in 1882 a large bronze of Cyzicus was found in the Catacombs of Domitilla on the Appian Way.[51] Note that our Cyzicus coin only carries graffiti on one side. If it were once a similarly wall mounted object, bust side outwards, as almost all catacomb coins were,[52] there would be little point in adding graffiti to the reverse. Indeed, even if it were mounted on a third century loculus it could still have remained exposed and received its graffiti in situ during later ages while the catacomb continued to be used.

In the British Museum's collection is a sculptural object which could be regarded as having a parallel history to this coin. This is in the form of a bust of Germanicus Caesar (15 BC – AD 19) that, although made in pagan times, has certainly remained exposed to scorn in later Christian centuries for its defacement not only includes a shattered nose and cut-marked neck but also a cross, cut deep into the hard basanite of its forehead. [fig. 8; bust of Germanicus].

CONS

Chapter Seven

CONSTANTINE TO CHRIST, THE CHRISTIAN AFTERMATH (ROMAN AND BYZANTINE EMPIRES, 4TH – 7TH CENTURY AD)

In the previous chapter we have seen that the earliest Biblical texts could abbreviate prominent sacred words. On coins too there was a long tradition of word abbreviation due to the restriction of physical space and, in addition, that more than one letter could be superimposed to make an interesting and emblematic monogram. These two traditions came together under Constantine the Great, the first Christian emperor, in his search for an emblematic visual identity for the new imperial faith.[53] As the word of God was central to the religion, a word became its first official logo or emblem. There were various choices of monogram available to early Christianity. [fig. 1a-e – suite of silver coins of 6th century Italy] To create a Christogram, the initials of Jesus' full Biblical name, IHCOC XPICTOC, the I and X could become ✱, while the first two letters of the messianic part of the name alone, X and P could be expressed as we have already met: ☧. An alternative monogram was to combine the Greek letters tau, T and rho, P ⳨. Like the chi-rho, the tau-rho monogram had already

Fig. 1a   *Fig. 1b*   *Fig. 1c*   *Fig. 1d*

existed in pre-Christian contexts – as we have already seen with the monogram on Herod's coinage of the first century BC (See chapter 3, fig. 2), possibly indicating the title 'tetrarch'. But to the Christians, tau-rho represented a staurogram (from the Greek for cross; stavros), since one can see a symbolic representation of crucifixion with the loop of the rho representing the head of the victim. The earliest Christian use seems to be on manuscripts of around AD 200 (dated paleographically – i.e. through writing style). If the palaeographic dating holds, it is certainly the oldest known form of Christian monogram.[54] In the 4th century Codex Sinaiticus we can see the same convention [fig. 2a] in Revelations 11:8 which contains the phrase "where Christ also was crucified": Ο ΠΟΥ ΚΑΙ Ο ΚϹ ΕϹ(ΤΡ)ω.3 Christ, ΚΡΙϹΤΟϹ, is contracted to ΚϹ and the word for crucified, ΕϹΤΑΥΡωΘΗ is contracted to ΕϹΤΡω;[55] again, appropriate to the subject, the adjacent tau and rho brought together by the contraction are superimposed. Codex Sinaiticus exhibits the next development by also reproducing the staurogram as a standalone decorative feature. They mark the end of Isaiah – an Old Testament book particularly dear to Christians due to its messianic prophesies. [fig. 2b] Constantine's coinage does eventually display the staurogram, but only right at the end of the reign. [fig. 5] It is a mintmark rather than the main design of the coin and thus chosen locally at the mint of

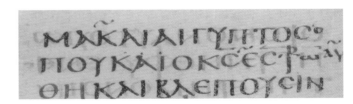

Fig. 2a

Antioch. It has been suggested that the staurogram could have been particularly associated with the Christians of the eastern parts of the Roman Empire. It seems to have been favoured in Coptic (Christian) Egypt, long used to the similar ankh symbol of eternal life.[56] For example, the staurogram, but not the chi-rho Christogram, is occasionally used in Codex Sinaiticus.[57]

Constantine explained his Christianity with a story set prior to his crucial battle against his rival Maxentius at the Milvian Bridge, outside Rome in AD 312. According to the contemporary Christian writer Lactantius, Constantine received a prophetic dream (*On the Deaths of the Persecutors* 44) although this was later confabulated by the emperor's official biographer into an additional (before the instructional dream) midday vision in the sun's rays before multiple witnesses (Eusebius, *Life of Constantine* 1.28-9). Although there is some measure of doubt due to unsatisfactory English translations of Lactantius,[58] the dream probably featured the staurogram (described by Lactantius as X turned sideways and bent over at the top, and by Bishop Eusebius as a cross-shaped trophy). This symbol he subsequently ordered to be painted on the shields of his troops just in time to aid their victory. Eusebius (*Life of Constantine* 1.29) also elaborates

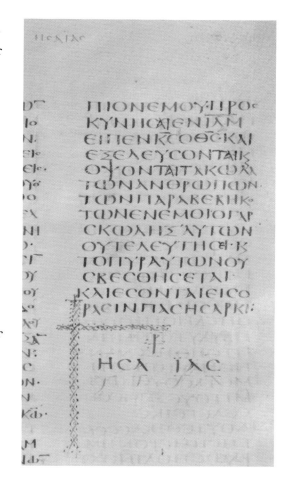

Fig. 2b

Fig. 3

that a cruciform standard was made representing the vision sign, the *labarum*. It was topped with a chi-rho monogram and this new device was also used as a badge on the emperor's helmet. Thus the vision-sign of an established Christian symbol (staurogram) had inspired a new personal symbol of Constantine's faith and victory, the Christogram. It is this latter symbol, possibly because of its direct political connection that proved more popular in fourth century AD material culture. It is seen as early as AD 315 on a silver medallion minted at Ticinum (Pavia in northern Italy). [fig. 4] Around this time is its first archaeological appearance. The city of Aquileia at the head of the Adriatic, has left us the finest monument to the first generation of Christians who could worship openly after the AD 313 Edict of Milan. This monument is in the form of the vast mosaic floor of the city's first basilica and which contains the dedicatory inscription of its Bishop Theodore. Along with the text is the earliest securely dated monumental Christogram, ☧; for the building work could hardly have started before the 313 edict and must have presumably been dedicated before the end of Theodore's tenure in 319. [fig. 5]

Fig. 4

The events of the Milvian Bridge, conflated with Constantine's new chi-rho victory badge, was probably also on the mind of a die engraver at the mint of Trier in AD 322 or 323 who embellished a bust of the emperor's son Crispus with a Christogram-emblazoned shield. [fig. 6]. Eusebius also noted a painting of the emperor above the façade of the imperial palace stabbing a serpent representing his enemies (*Life of Constantine* 3.3). He goes on to note Isaiah 27:1:

Fig. 6

The lord will punish with his sword…Leviathan the coiling serpent;
he will slay the monster of the sea.

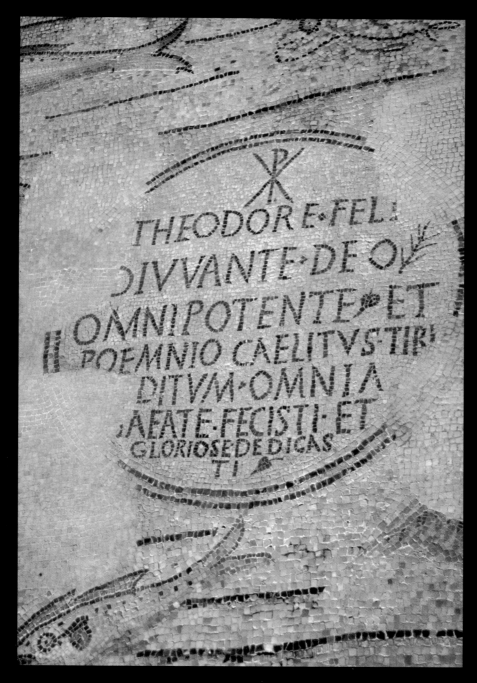

Fig. 5

89

The imperial palace was in fact a new-build at Byzantium, now invested as Constantinople, the new Rome. This foundation was a direct result of the defeat of the pagan emperor Licinius by Constantine by a sea assault on Chrysopolis across the Bosphorus, opposite Byzantium, in AD 324. The defeat of this Roman 'Leviathan' Licinius gave Constantine mastery over the whole Roman world. By AD 327 the city also had its own branch of the imperial mint, and one of its first coin types was of Constantine's Christianised standard piercing a serpent; perhaps alluding to Constantine's action in the official painting seen by Eusebius. [fig. 7]

Fig. 7

Fig. 8

Constantine was a Christian emperor in a then predominantly pagan empire. His coinage carries only passing references to what would have been regarded by the majority as his personal cult in a multicultural society. Upon his death in AD 337, Constantine was deified just like a traditional pagan emperor. Yet the coinage commemorating this event managed to add in Biblical elements. [fig. 8: gold Constantine deification coin] On this type the bust of Constantine is veiled with a fold of toga pulled over the head in the proper funereal pagan manner. However, the reverse shows the emperor ascending to heaven in a chariot, stretching out to reach the hand of God. It is echoing the description of the prophet Elijah's ascent to heaven in a supernatural chariot (2 Kings 2:11).

It was instead left to succeeding generations to make Christianity the central theme on Roman coins as the Roman Empire edged towards a fully Christian society over the course of the fourth century and beyond. It was the exact mid point of the fourth century before Constantine's vision was illustrated with its divine message: HOC SIGNO VICTOR ERIS (by this sign you will be victorious). [fig. 9] This type appeared in the midst of the civil war of AD 350-3 when all sides were naturally trying to claim the legitimate succession to Constantine through his victorious badge. Surprisingly the most notable coin imagery was employed not by the embattled legitimate emperor Constantius II, the son of Constantine, but by his rivals Magnentius in the west and (more briefly) Vetranio in the area of the Danube. His principal rival produced the first Christogram as the main coin type [fig. 10: Coin of Magnentius]. It appears in its fullest form; flanked by alpha and omega. The Biblical reference to the use of the first and last letters of the Greek alphabet has already been discussed. Also noted in the previous chapter is the pre-Christian use of the monogram as a rho-chi in the word archon, αρχων, head of a city council and ruler of their community. Recent research has noted that the full Christogram symbol can still be read both ways, chi-rho and rho-chi. The latter way combined with the alpha and omega creates APXW, 'I rule', an appropriate message for both God and emperor.[59]

But what of that quintessential symbol of Christianity, the instrument of the crucifixion itself? At the beginning of the fourth century the cross itself is presumed to have

Fig. 9

Fig. 10

Fig. 11

represented a shameful and humiliating death (Fig. 11: Alexamenos graffito) and only seems to have gradually become widely acceptable in <u>official</u> art over the succeeding decades. Indeed the first steps to the rehabilitation of the cross as the definitive symbol of Christianity can be credited to Constantine's mother, Helena around AD 326. St Helena became the world's first Biblical archaeologist by travelling at an advanced age to Jerusalem and ordering the search and miraculous discovery of the True Cross (the cross upon which Jesus was executed): the start of the medieval relic business. [fig. 12; Helena medallion] Constantine did his bit too. He discontinued crucifixion in favour of another extremely cruel form of capital punishment once also used by Herod the Great and that would become characteristic of the medieval world: burning at the stake. Small crosses do appear on Constantinian coinage, but they are difficult to interpret as their simple shapes could be mintmarks chosen by the mint official to distinguish a production run and which may or may not have Christian significance. An unequal-armed cross on a coin of AD 335 does appear to look quite deliberately Christian. [fig. 13] It is very late in Constantine's reign and interestingly from the city of Aquileia with its early basilica. An equal armed cross is found on a coin from the mint of Ticinum (Pavia, also in nothern Italy) as early as AD 316. [fig. 14] One reason why it might well be an early Christian symbol is that the mint itself as already seen had

Fig. 12

Fig. 13

Fig. 14

just produced a medallion with an unequivocally Christian Christogram in AD 315. If this cross of AD 316 was intentionally Christian it might at first seem incongruous next to the coin's reverse type of the sun god Sol, with legend SOLI INVICTO COMITI (the invincible sun, the [emperor's] companion). Septimius Severus (AD 193-211) had brought the cult of the sun god to Rome from the east and Sol Invictus appears on Severan coinage from AD 197. Sol's head radiates solar rays and hand is raised in gesture of salute as a god might well do at the point of his manifestation to the world. In the case of a solar god, this point of manifestation was sunrise and as the cult grew over the course of the third century AD, the concept of the rising sun from the east was often encapsulated by the alternative coin motto frequently used for the type: Oriens. Sol sometimes carries a globe in his other hand or alternatively a whip to drive his chariot across the sky, a traditional role of Apollo of whom Sol could be considered one specialised aspect. However, the concept of the one true deity who could be worshipped to the exclusion of all others and who rises unconquered by death in the east (reborn annually on the 25th December) could also appeal to quite another religious group: the Christians. When we eventually come to it, for they do take their time to appear, the earliest images representing Christ himself appear unfamiliar to the modern viewer. Beardless, youthful, delicately handsome and androgynous if not often quite effeminate; in other words distinctively Apolline and sometimes identified as Christos Helios (using the Greek equivalent of Sol).

Interestingly, the cross was the symbol of choice for some of the earliest overtly Christian coinage occurring outside the Roman Empire. This was at Aksum; the only part of sub-tropical Africa to produce its own coinage in antiquity. The first Aksumite king to convert was Ezana, sometime around the year AD 330, an event recorded in Roman history a few decades later and which provides one of the few fixed points in establishing the regnal sequence and rough chronology to an otherwise a-historical ancient civilization. Just like his contemporary, Constantine the Great, who became an Orthodox saint, Ezana too came to be canonised by his own church. The imagery of Aksumite gold coinage centred on the king and the royal bust (in different headgear) was carried on both sides. It is the legends which show the striking change [fig. 15], heralding the format of coinages of later medieval Europe punctuated with crosses. The Aksumite coins' Greek legend

Fig. 15

punctuation also occurs between syllables; reflecting the underlying translation from the ancient Ethiopic Ge'ez (still used as the liturgical language of the Ethiopian and Eritrean Orthodox Churches) and having the effect of peppering it with crosses. More elaborate, larger crosses began to appear as the main type on lower denomination coins. These silver and bronze coins often

Fig. 16

had their most important design features, like the cross, gilded: an extraordinarily detailed addition to an otherwise mass produced item. This form of decoration is unique in ancient coins.

The cross waited much longer to take its place as a Roman coin type in its own right and by then a new century had dawned. [fig. 16] Around this time the depiction of the Crucifixion was being added to the vocabulary of Christian art. The dilemma of early Christian artists to show the central incident in the Gospel message without dwelling on the humiliation of the criminal execution is neatly expressed in a surviving ivory casket panel from the early fifth century AD. [fig. 17] With the absence of suffering, Jesus is triumphant in death. Contemporary numismatic expressions of this triumph could still involve the Christian symbols juxtaposed with Victory herself. [fig. 18] But like the remaining pagans of Rome, Victory's days were numbered too and in the following century she had become de-gendered to a flat-chested angel. [fig. 19] When Jesus is asked about the fate of the remarried once they reach heaven and meet previous partners, he points to the genderless nature of the heavenly host:

When the dead rise, they will be neither marry or be given in marriage; they will be like the angels in

Fig. 17

Fig. 18

Fig. 19

heaven (Mark 12:25)

The cross became such a staple feature of Byzantine coinage that a sort of coin war manifested itself during the titanic struggle between Byzantium and the rising Islamic Empire. The embattled emperor Heraclius (AD 610-41) raised the arms race of crosses with a type that sported no less than seven; a main cross on steps reverse plus an obverse of the emperor standing shoulder to shoulder with his sons wearing or bearing six more [fig. 20]. The response came later in the century with a near copy of the coin type by the Caliph 'Abd al-Malik (AD 685-705, or AH 65-86). The same emperor and sons image is repeated but

Fig. 20

Fig. 21

shorn of crosses. [fig. 21] The reverse has been left as a pole on steps. Similar treatment was given to Byzantine monuments in conquered areas: most famously the great cross reliefs in the Hagia Sofia which can still be seen with their crossbars neatly chipped out.

The figure of Christ himself had appeared in art much earlier than this and even before the Crucifixion scene there is a Romano-British floor mosaic with a bust apparently representing Jesus. [fig. 22] It was created in the fourth century and, with the early fifth century downfall of the Roman-Britain, beyond Roman jurisdiction by the time sacred images were proscribed for floor use in AD 427.[60] In fact we can be sure of a mid-fourth century date as it appears stylistically similar to, and was even possibly inspired by, the Christogram coin of AD 353. [fig. 10] Comparison with the mosaic shows that the artist simply had to turn the imperial bust with its pudding bowl haircut and superimpose it onto the reverse Christogram. The expected alpha and omega have been replaced by the pagan symbols of the afterlife: pomegranates.[61] There is the distinct possibility that Jesus

Fig. 22

Fig. 23

Fig. 24

first appears on a coin in the mid-fifth century as a nimbate (haloed) figure in the background embracing the emperor and empress. The imperial couple are also haloed, reminding us that this characteristic attribute of Christian art actually began as an imperial device.[62] However, Jesus's halo is different – the detail is on a tiny scale but it can be seen that the nimbus is marked out by containing a cross within, his distinctive *nimbus cruciger*. [fig. 23]

Fig. 25a

When this marriage scene type is repeated on a coin of Anastasius I (AD 491-518 – married to Ariadne, his predecessor's widow in 491and often regarded as the first 'Byzantine' as opposed to Roman emperor after the

Fig. 25b

fall of west) a subtle but telling change had occurred. Only the background figure of Jesus is haloed (with the same nimbus cruciger as the first appearance); those of Anastasius and Ariadne are not. [fig. 24] In addition, gone is the Apolline clean-shaven late Roman Christ and we are given the first – albeit indistinct – glimpse of a more familiar bearded figure; a new epoch in the depiction of Jesus in art had begun.

However, it was to be another two centuries before the central figure of the Gospels would become a main coin type, well into the Byzantine period proper, and in fact displacing the imperial bust from the front of the coin. [fig. 25a & b] Instead we are initially faced with a choice of two individuals on the coinage of an emperor who had two reigns; Justinian II (AD 685-95 and 705-11). In the second reign the previously unassailable ruler had been replaced by an outraged and vengeful victim of torture (in an unsuccessful bid to discourage his return to power his tongue was slit and his nose cropped, but of course this was never indicated on the coin effigies). On the first reign coinage Jesus appears as Zeus-like godhead with flowing hair that would go on to become the familiar Byzantine figure of Christ Pantocrator (almighty).[63] The image would overshadow later Byzantine coinage to the extent of driving all references to the emperor entirely from the base metal denomination by the turn of the millennium [fig. 26]. It is possible that, like the Constantine Labarum type, this is another example of an original artwork from the entrance to the imperial palace at Constantinople transferred to coinage.[64] The second type of Justinian II shows Jesus as a haggard, curly-haired, unshaven Levantine monk (the 'suffering' or 'Syrian' Christ to art historians).[65] This short-lived but interesting alternative image only appeared on coinage of the troubled second reign of Justinian II, who had by then experienced the privations of a fall from grace and the desperate bid to regain power. Both busts are superimposed before a cross (as the Hinton St Mary bust had been in front of a Christogram), holding up their right hands in the traditional gesture of address, and both – regardless of whether they represent the human or divine nature of Jesus – hold the Bible.

Fig. 26

ΠΙΟΝΕΜΟΥ ΠΡΟϹ
ΚΥΝΗϹΑΙ ΕΝΙ ΑΜ
ΕΙΠΕΝ ΚϹ Ο ΘϹ ΚΑΙ
ΕΞΕΛΕΥϹΟΝΤΑΙ Κ
ΟΨΟΝΤΑΙ ΤΑ ΚΩΛΑ
ΤΩΝ ΑΝΘΡΩΠΩΝ
ΤΩΝ ΠΑΡΑΒΕΒΗΚ
ΤΩΝ ΕΝ ΕΜΟΙ ΟΓΑΡ
ϹΚΩΛΗΞ ΑΥΤΩΝ
ΟΥ ΤΕΛΕΥΤΗϹΕ Κ
ΤΟ ΠΥΡ ΑΥΤΩΝ ΟΥ
ϹΒΕϹΘΗϹΕΤΑΙ
ΚΑΙ ΕϹΟΝΤΑΙ ΕΙϹ Ο
ΡΑϹΙΝ ΠΑϹΗ ϹΑΡΚΙ

ΗϹΑ ΙΑϹ

Appendices

Money related passages in the New Testament and their original Greek terms as they appear in the Codex Sinaiticus (http://codexsinaiticus.org)

(Matthew 5:26)	…you will not get out until you have paid the last quadrans (ECXATO KOΔPANTHN)
(Matthew 10:9)	"Do not take along any gold or silver or copper in your belts"
(Matthew 10:29)	Are not two sparrows sold for an assarion (ACCAPIOY)?
(Matthew 17:24)	…the collectors of the two-drachma (ΔIΔPAXMA) temple tax came to Peter…
(Matthew 17:27)	Take the first fish you catch; open its mouth and you will find a four-drachma piece (CTATHPA = stater)
(Matthew 20:9 & 13)	…each received a denarius…Didn't you agree to work for a denarius (ΔHNAPIOY)?
(Matthew 22:19)	"Show me the coin used for paying the tax." They brought him a denarius (ΔHNAPION)…
(Matthew 25:16)	The man who had received the five talents went at once and put his money to work and gained five more (ΠENTE TAΛANTA)
(Matthew 26:15)	…so they counted out for him thirty pieces of silver (· Λ · APΓYPIA; note: Λ is also the Greek numeral for 30)
(Mark 6:37)	That would take more than two hundred denarii (ΔHNAPIΩN ΔIAKOCIΩN)!
(Mark 12:15)	"Bring me a denarius (ΔHNAPION) and let me look at it."
(Mark 12:42)	Many rich people threw in large amounts. But a poor widow came and put in two lepta, worth a quadrans (ΛEΠTA ΔYO O ECTI KOΔPAN).
(Mark 14:5)	It could have been sold for more than 300 denarii (ΔHNAPIΩN TPIAKOCIΩN)…
(Luke 3:14)	– be content with your pay [OΨΩNIOIC = stipend]
(Luke 10;35)	The next day he took out two denarii (ΔYO ΔHNAPIA) and gave them to the innkeeper
(Luke 12:6)	Are not five sparrows sold for two assaria (ACCAPIΩN ΔYO)?
(Luke 12:57-59)	… you will not get out until you have paid the last lepton (ECXATON ΛEΠTON)
(Luke 15:8)	…suppose a woman has ten drachmae and loses one (ΔPAXMAC EXOYCA ΔEKA EAN AΠOΛECH ΔPAXMH)
(Luke 19:13)	So he called ten of his servants and gave them ten minas (ΔEKA MNAC)
(Acts 19:19)	When they calculated the value of the scrolls, the total came to fifty thousand pieces of silver (APΓYPIOY)

Further Reading

J. Bardill, 2012	*Constantine, Divine Emperor of the Golden Age* (Cambridge University Press)
J. Barton, 2010	*The Bible: The Basics* (Routledge, London)
D. Hendin, 2010	*Guide to Biblical Coins* (Amphora, New York)
2012	*Cultural Change: Jewish, Christian and Islamic Coins of the Holy Land* (American Numismatic Society, New York)
L. W. Hurtado, 2007	*The Earliest Christian Artifacts: Manuscripts and Christian Origins* (William B Eerdmans Publishing Co., Grand Rapids / Cambridge)
D. M. Jacobson and N. Kokkinos 2012	*Judaea and Rome in Coins, 65 BCE – 135 CE* (London, Spink)
D. M. Jacobson 2013	The Lily and the Rose : A Review of some Hasmonean Coin Types, *Near Eastern Archaeology 76:1, pp16-27*
Nikos Kokkinos (ed.), 2007	*The World of the Herods*. Volume 1 (Oriens et Occidens. Band 14), (Stuttgart, Franz Steiner)
W. Metcalf (ed), 2012	*The Oxford Handbook of Greek and Roman Coinage* (OUP, New York)
D. C. Parker, 2010	*Codex Sinaiticus: the story of the world's oldest bible*, (London : British Library & Peabody, Mass.)
J. R. Porter 2007	*Jesus Christ* (London, Duncan Baird Publishers)
M. Price, 1975	*Coins and the Bible* (S. Walker Ltd, Hinckley, Leicestershire)
Y. Meshorer 2001	*A Treasury of Jewish Coins* (Jerusalem-Nyack)

Online sources

British Museum collections	www.britishmuseum.org/research/search_the_collection_database.aspx
Codex Sinaiticus (Cod. Sin.)	http://codexsinaiticus.org/en

Other Bibliographical citations

Ancient authors:

(Note: New International Version used for English Biblical translations wherever possible)

Dio Cassius	*Roman History* (vol. 8 = E. Cary trans.; Loeb Classical Library, 1989)
Eusebius	*Life of Constantine* (Cameron and Hall trans.; Oxford University Press, 1999)
	Ecclesiastical History (C. F. Cruse trans.; Rough Draft Printing 2011)
Josephus	*Jewish Antiquities* (R. Marcus and A. Wikgren, trans: Loeb Classical Library, 1998 reprint)
	Jewish War (H. St. J. Thackeray trans.; Loeb Classical Library, 1971)
Lactantius	*The Works of Lactantius* (Trans: W. Fletcher trans.; Edinburgh 1871)
Petronius	*Satyricon* (J P Sullivan, trans: Penguin Classics, London 2011)
Pliny the Younger	Letters, Volume II: Books 8-10. Panegyricus (Betty Radice trans.; Loeb Classical Library, 1969)
SHA	Lives of the Later Caesars (A. & A. Birley trans.; Penguin Classics, 1976)

Modern authors:

P. Bruun, 1997	'The victorious signs of Constantine: a reappraisal', in *Numismatic Chronicle*, pp. 41-60.
R. S. Bagnall, 2009	*Early Christian Books in Egypt* (Princeton University Press)
M. Barasch, 1994	'The Ruling and the Suffering Christ: Physiognomic Typology on Justinian Coins' in *Imago Homnis, Studies in the Language of Art* (New York University Press)
A. R. Bellinger, 1966	*Catalogue of the Byzantine Coins in the Dumbarton Oaks Collection and in the Whittemore Collection. Vol. 1: Anastasius I to Maurice, 491–602.* (Dumbarton Oaks, Washington D.C.)
K. Butcher 2004	*Coinage in Roman Syria* (Royal Numismatic Society, London 2004)
K. Butcher and M. Ponting 2013	*The Metallurgy of Roman Silver Coinage: From the Reforms of Nero to the Reform of Trajan* (Cambridge University Press)
A. Cameron and S. G. Hall 1999	*Eusebius, Life of Constantine* (Clarendon Press, Oxford)
A. D. DeConick 2006	*The Original Gospel of Thomas in Translation* (London, Bloomsbury Publishing PLC)

J. Elsner 1998	*Imperial Rome and Christian Triumph* (Oxford University Press)
M. F. Hendy 1985	*Studies in the Byzantine Monetary Economy c.300-1450* (Cambridge University Press)
L. Mildenburg 1984	*The Coinage of the Bar Kokhba War* (Verlag Sauerländer, Aarau/Frankfurt/Salzburg)
S. Moorhead 2005	'The Hinton St. Mary head of Christ and a coin of Magnentius', in N. Crummy (ed.), *Image, Craft and the Classical World. Essays in Honour of Donald Bailey and Catherine Johns* (Éditions Monique Mergoil, Montagnac)
S. Moorhead & D. Stuttard 2012	*The Romans Who Shaped Britain,* (London, Thames & Hudson)
T. Opper 2008	*Hadrian: Empire and Conflict* (London, British Museum Press)
P. Parsons 2007	*City of the Sharp-Nosed Fish: Greek Papyri Beneath the Egyptian Sand Reveal a Long-Lost World* (Orion Books Ltd, London)
S. Pearce 2008	'The Hinton St Mary Mosaic Pavement: Christ or Emperor?' *Britannia*, Vol. 39 (2008), pp. 193-218
R. Reece 1981	'Roman monetary impact on the Celtic world – thoughts and problems.' In B. W. Cunliffe (ed.) *Coinage and society in Britain and Gaul: some current problems* (Council for British Archaeology, York)
R. Reece 2002	*The Coinage of Roman Britain,* (Stroud, Tempus)
W. Smith and S. Cheetham 1908	*A Dictionary of Christian Antiquities* (John Murray (pub.), London)
J. Spier 2007	*Picturing the Bible, the Earliest Christian Art* (Yale University Press, New Haven and London)
J. M. C. Toynbee 1986	*Roman Medallions* (with introduction by W. E. Metcalf) (American Numismatic Society, New York)
Y. Yadin 1971	*Bar-Kokhba: The Rediscovery of the Legendary Hero of the Second Jewish Revolt Against Rome* (New York: Random House)

Endnotes

1. The 'wave offering' was an offering of a sheaf of barley made by Jewish priests. Leviticus 23:9-11 The Lord said to Moses "Speak to the Israelites and say to them: 'When you enter the land I am going to give you and you reap its harvest, bring to the priest a sheaf of the first grain of harvest. He is to wave the sheaf before the Lord so it will be accepted on your behalf; the priest is to wave it on the day after the Sabbath.'"

2. Table after Hendin (2001)

3. Translation from the New Revised Standard Version, Catholic Edition.

3a. See Jaccobson 2013 for discussion of flower types on Hasmonean coins.

4. See for example Porter 2007, 60-1

5. Strangely Josephus contradicts himself in another work, the *Jewish War* 1.401. This places the start of building work earlier, occurring in Herod's 15th year (= 23/22 BC), making a more problematic chronology which would seem too early for Jesus's ministry.

6. The observation supposedly made by Augustus, that it was "better to be Herod's pig than his son" (Macrobius, *Saturnalia*, book II, IV, 11) was recorded by a fifth century writer as part of a later Christian tradition concerning the episode of the massacre of the innocents.

7. See Hendin 2010, p.231-2

8. See RPC I, p.678 for latest scholarly discussion of Herod's coinage

9. RPC I does not consider the half-prutah, but they are listed by Hendin

10. For recent discussion of the coinage of Antipas see: RPC I, p.679-80

11. See RPC I, p.570, contra Hendin *Cultural Change: Jewish, Christian, and Islamic coins of the Holy Land* (New York, American Numismatic Society 2012), p.40

12. This traditional order of the New Testament canon is sometimes termed *Augustinian priority* in recognition that it dates back at least as far as the days of the fourth century AD 'church father' St Augustine of Hippo (AD 354-430)

13. For a concise recent history of modern Biblical studies see Barton 2010

14. See DeConick *The Original Gospel of Thomas in Translation* (London, Bloomsbury Publishing PLC, 2006). Another 20th century discovery was the (Gnostic) Gospel of Judas, another non-canonical work. See R. Kasser, M. Meyer and G. Wurst, *The Gospel of Judas* (National Geographic Society, Washington DC, 2006).

15. Inscriptions recording Diocletian's Prices Edict of AD 301 show the 2:1 value ratio of orichalcum brass to copper

16. For example the Greek version of the *Res Gestae* (the great inscription detailing the deeds of Augustus set up throughout the empire), converted sums of *sestertii* from the Latin text into *denaria* (denarii)

17. It was quite probably uneconomical to make such shipments, but there might also have been less demand

for such a coin anyway. See F. McIntosh and S. Moorhead, 'Roman *quadrantes* found in Britain in light of recent discoveries recorded with the Portable Antiquities Scheme' *British Numismatic Journal* vol. 81 (2011), pp. 223-9. The Romano-British marketplace might not have wanted to conduct monetary transactions as such a low level even if it could do so. There are two factors other than coin supply that might determine how low a denomination is needed in a society. A society that is less monetised might carry out degrees of low level transactions through the direct trading or barter (e.g. the medieval kingdoms of England and Scotland lacked base metal small change). On the other hand a less economically developed society might need smaller denominations due to a lower cost of living. One authority on Roman coinage (Reece 2002, 117) has cited a relatively modern example of Malta during its time in the British Empire which had small change tariffed at fractions of a farthing, the lowest pre-decimal coin available in contemporary Britain.

18. The revival of the term assarion centuries later as a Byzantine copper coin under the emperors Andronicus II and Michael IX (1295-1320) was probably a result of these well-known passages in Matthew and Luke.

19. See Butcher 2004, ch.3.10, 'The date of the introduction of the denarius and aureus to Syria', pp.192-5. Only two pre-revolt contexts are noted: at Qumrân and Mount Carmel. The latter contained at least 160 denarii of Augustus minted at Lyon, alongside over 4,000 Tyrian tetradrachms and didrachms (the hoard was not fully recorded).

20. Although the Levant's southern neighbour of Roman Egypt produced its own coinage, it had a closed currency circulation that effectively set it apart financially from the rest of the region and features little in this period.

21. Data from M. Speidel, *Journal of Roman Studies* vol. 82 1992, p.106

22. Reece 1981, 27-8

23. Interestingly, a Jacobean labourer could expect the equivalent of eight silver pennies on a daily basis. Data from J. E. T. Rogers, *A History of Agriculture and Prices in England, vol.V, 1583-1702 (Oxford 1887)*. Unlike the Biblical situation, this was less than the contemporary daily wage of a soldier (the traditional King's shilling, i.e. 12 pence).

24. Reece 2002, p.112

25. For army pay scales see Speidel, p. 106

26. Diocletian's price edict of AD 301 stipulated 25 denarii as a labourer's daily wage

27. The property qualification of the lower level of aristocracy, an equestrian was 100,000 denarii /drachmae

28. For in-depth discussion of the Temple tax see Hendin 2001, p.262 and 420-9

29. For a thorough overview of the various silver standards of Roman Provincial coinage during the first century BC / AD see pt. II pp.354ff. of Butcher and Ponting 2013

30. It was only with changes to the silver content of the denarius during the AD 60s that western and eastern silver became more interchangeable and the denarius became more prevalent in the Levant. Butcher and Ponting 2013, see especially 'Towards a history of provincial silver standards', pp.525-7.

31. See RPC 1's introduction to the mint of Tyre, pp. 655-6, and p.7 of A. Burnett, 'The Herodian Coinage Viewed against the Wider Perspective of Roman Coinage' in Jacobson and Kokkinos (2012). Butcher and Ponting (2013) can point to another factor in the disappearance of the Tyrian shekel: the change in the silver standard of the

Roman denarius under Nero.

32. Although there are a number of non-canonical traditions for the death of Judas Iscariot, there are two different descriptions in the Bible itself of how Judas Iscariot met his end – either (Matthew 27:3–10) Judas returned the money to the priests and then hanged himself (the priests using the money to buy the Potter's Field) or (Acts 1:18) Judas used the money to buy a field but fell headfirst in the field and his guts burst and so the field was known as the Field of Blood (Akeldama).

33. A similar story to the Parable of the Talents is found in Luke 19:13-27, but using a different weight: the mina. Though these parables seem very similar there are significant differences (such as the equal distribution of minas in Luke's parable). The two parables may come from separate sources and there are also links to the non-canonical Gospel of the Hebrews and the contemporary writer Josephus.

34. The date of the foundation is not without contention but does seem to be in advance of the conflict to judge by the order it is recorded in ancient sources (Cassius Dio 69.12). See Mildenburg (1984), p.104, or H. Gitler in the *Oxford Handbook* (see further reading), p.492-3. In his thorough examination of the war and its coinage, Mildenburg views the creation of Aelia to have occurred in advance of the war and hence been one of the causes of the conflict along with the circumcision ban.

35. See Yadin (1971) and also Opper (2008), pp.89-97

36. Yadin (1971), p.178

37. For summary of the debate on the Ark-like object on this coinage, see p. 56 of Amar Z. 2009–2010, 'The Shewbread Table on the Mattathias Antigonus: A Reconsideration.' *INJ* 17:48–58. Contra: Barag, D., 1987, 'The Table for Shewbread and the Facades of the Temple on the Bar Kokhba Coins, *Qadmoniot* 77-8.

38. Mildenberg 1984, p.98, n.272

39. ibid, p.98-9, although Mildenberg feels he can give an even closer date range of AD 130-2.

40. Loeb trans.

41. This Jewish community was certainly still in evidence in the 1st century BC when Lucius Valerius Flaccus was Roman propraetor and governor of the province of Asia. Flaccus passed a law in c.62 BC forbidding the export of gold collected by the Jewish communities of Asia to send to Jerusalem. Apamea is mentioned specifically by Cicero (pro Flacco 66-69) as one of these communities, and the quantity mentioned, a little under 100 Roman pounds of gold, was a significant amount: about 32-33kg.

42. B. M. Metzger, (1991). Manuscripts of the Greek Bible: An Introduction to Palaeography, Oxford: Oxford University Press, p. 76.

43. Parker (2010), pp.61-3. Parker uses the cost information from Diocletian's Price Edict of AD 301, which also includes the relative cost of gold. The contemporary gold piece to the Codex Sinaiticus was the solidus with a target weight of 4.55g (1/72nd of a Roman pound of gold), produced after AD 309.

44. Hurtado (2006), p.112

45. See Hurtado (2006), p.114-5 for the good omen of Jesus's name seen in Genesis 14.14

46. Parsons (2007), pp.205-6

47. For non-Christian uses of the chi-rho in ancient texts see Hurtado (2006), p.137, including P. Mur 164a, a papyrus from a context relating to the 2nd Jewish revolt (AD 132-5)

48. Price (1975), p.28

49. See Toynbee (1986), p.120, citing C. Serafini, 'Saggio

intorno alle monete e medaglioni antichi ritrovati nelle catacombe di Panfilo sulla Via Salaria Vetus in Roma (*Scritti in onore di Bartolomeo Nogara raccolti in occasione del suo lxx anno,* 1937, pp.421-443)

50. P. Serafin & M. C. Molinari, 'Monete e Medaglie dal Centro di Roma e dal suburbia nella letteratura numismatica' in *I territori di Roma, storie, popolazioni, geografie, Convegno di Studi delle Università romane.* Società geografica Italiana, Roma 2000, pp. 257-272.

51. Reported by G. B. de Rossi, in *Bullettino Di Archeologia Cristiana* (1883), p.78 (available online at http://periodici. librari.beniculturali.it). The coin was an issue of Gordian III (AD 238-44).

52. See Toynbee (1986), p.120

53. See also Bruun (1997) and appendix 2 ('Earliest Christian Symbols on Roman Coins') of Metcalf (2012), pp.663-6

54. It is a fragment including Luke 14.27 (P. Bodmer XIV), see Hurtado (2006), p.140-3; pl.4-5. For a recent work reassessing the dating of the earliest Christian papyri see Bagnall (2009).

55. Cf. Smith and Cheetham (1908: 1313)

56. One celebrated 4th century AD Egyptian stone inscription from Armant carries staurograms alongside ankhs. See Hurtado (2006) pp.143-4, however, he does not feel that the staurogram actually developed from the ankh (2006, p.146). Bardill (2012), p.189 and 192 shows an imperial porphyry sarcophagus in Istanbul with an ankh symbol with chi-rho in its loop. Although from a later age it does demonstrate an affinity between it and Christian symbolism in Late Antiquity.

57. Smith and Cheetham (1908), p.1311

58. See Bardill (2012), pp.161-2. He gives the original Latin: *transversa X littera, summo capite circumflexo.*

59. Moorhead and Stuttard (2012), p.193

60. See Pearce (2008)

61. Moorhead (2005), pp.209-212

62. Nimbate imperial effigies can be seen on Roman coins from the beginning of the fourth century AD, although in fact the earliest appearance was on coins of the second century emperor Antoninus Pius (AD 138-61). See for example British Museum specimen R.13638, viewable online.

63. The finest representation of Zeus had in fact come to Constantinople in the art collection of one of the courtiers of Theodosius II (AD 402-50): the 4th century BC Zeus of Olympia by the artist Phidias, one of the seven wonders of the ancient world. See Elsner (1998), p.189.

64. Hendy (1985), pp.97-8.

65. Barasch (1994), pp.112-8.

Index of Illustrations

2.04 Gold coin of Antiochus IV Epiphanes (Syria, 174-165 BC), diademed head of Antiochus IV, right, with reverse of Zeus seated, left, holding eagle and sceptre, with inscription ΒΑΣΙ ΛΕΩΣ~ΑΝΤΙΟΧΟΥ~ΘΕΟΥ~ΕΠΙΦΑΝΟΥΣ~ΝΙΚΗ ΦΟΡΟΥ (King Antiochus, God manifest, bearing victory), 1909,0110.1 (Max diam. 21mm)

2.05 Mattathias punishing idolatry, etching and engraving from the volume of Apocrypha from Macklin's Bible, published in 1816, 1859,0312.211

2.06 Judas Maccabeus giving commands to cleanse the Temple, Flemish print of 1585, after Gerard Groenning, 1968,1018.1.211

2.07 Silver coin of Diodotus Tryphon, 140-142 BC, minted at Antioch on the Orontes, diademed head of Tryphon, right, with reverse of spiked Macedonian helmet adorned with wild goat's horn and medallions containing eagle and panther, with inscription ΒΑΣΙΛΕΩΣ~ΤΡΥΦΩΝΟΣ~ΑΥΤΟΚΡΑΤΟΡΟΣ, 1858,1124.80 (Max diam. 29mm)

2.08 Silver coin of Antiochus VII Sidetes (Syria, 138-129 BC), diademed head of Antiochus VII, right, with reverse of Athena holding Nike, spear and resting on shield, with inscription ΒΑΣΙΛΕΩΣ~ΑΝΤΙΟΧΟΥ~ΕΥΕΡΓΕΤΟΥ, 1908,1210.188 (Max diam. 33mm)

2.09-10 Tyrian silver: shekel 1962,0408.1 (59 BC) and half-shekel 1897,0104.506 (undated; 1st century BC / AD). Head of Melkart-Heracles with reverse of eagle and club. (Max diams. 29mm & 23mm)

2.11 Bronze coin of John Hyrcanus I, 135-104BC (prutah), minted at Jerusalem, inscription Yehohanan the High Priest and the Council of the Jews, within oak wreath and reverse of double cornucopia adorned with ribbons, and pomegranate between horns, 1908,0110.47 (Max diam. 15mm)

2.12 Bronze coin of John Hyrcanus I 135-104BC (½ prutah), minted at Jerusalem, lily, with reverse of palm branch and inscription Yehohanan the High Priest and head of the Council of the Jews, 1908,0110.189 (Max diam. 12mm)

2.13 John Hyrcanus I 135-104BC (double prutah), minted at Jerusalem, crested helmet, with reverse of double cornucopia, adorned with ribbons; surrounded by the inscription Yehohanan the High Priest and head of the Council of the Jews, 1908,0110.183 (Max diam. 18mm)

2.14 Bronze coin of Judas Aristobulus, 104-103 BC, (prutah), minted at Jerusalem, inscription within a laurel-wreath, Yehudah the High Priest and the Council of the Jews, with reverse of double cornucopia adorned with ribbons, pomegranate between horns, 1908,0110.83 (Max diam. 16mm)

2.15 Bronze coin of Alexander Jannaeus, 103-76 BC, minted at Jerusalem, inscription within a wreath, Yonatan the High Priest and the Council of Jews, and reverse of double cornucopia adorned with ribbons, pomegranate between horns, 1908,0110.172 (Max diam. 16mm)

2.16 Bronze coin of Alexander Jannaeus, 103-76 BC, minted at Jerusalem, anchor with inscription ΒΑΣΙΛΕΩΣ ΑΛΕΞΑΝΔΡ[ΟΥ], with reverse of star and inscription Yehonatan the King, 1908,1111.28 (Max diam. 14mm)

2.17 Bronze coin of Alexander Jannaeus, 103-76BC, minted in Jerusalem, anchor with inscription [ΒΑΣΙΛΕΩΣ Α]ΛΕΞΑΔΡΟ[Υ], with reverse of lily and inscription Yehonatan the King, 1862,0721.5 (Max diam. 15mm)

2.18 Bronze coin of John Hyrcanus II, 67-40 BC, minted at Jerusalem, inscription within a wreath; parts of anchor/circle design remain from overstruck coin, with reverse of double cornucopia adorned with ribbons, pomegranate between horns; parts of lily and hebrew inscription remain from earlier coin. Inscriptions, (undertype = Alexander Jannaeus with same inscriptions as above), Yehonatan the King, with reverse of Yehonatan the High Priest and the Council of the Jews : 1908,0110.147 (Max diam. 16mm)

2.19 Bilingual bronze coin of Mattatayah Antigonus, 40-37BC, minted at Jerusalem, double cornucopia and ivy wreath designs. Inscriptions: Mattatiyah the High Priest and the council of the Jews), BAC[ΙΛ]ΕΩΣ ΑΝΤΙΓΟΝΟΥ, 1908,0110.214 (Max diam. 23mm)

2.20 Bronze coin of Mattatayah Antigonus, 40-37BC, menorah with inscription [ΒΑΣΙΛ]ΕΩΣ ΑΝΤ[ΙΓΟΝΟΥ], with reverse of Showbread table, 1888,0512.29 (Max diam. 18mm)

2.21 Bronze coin of Antiochus VII, 138-129 BC, (and John Hyrcanus?), minted at Jerusalem(?), 132-130 BC, lily and reverse of anchor design with inscription, ΒΑΣΙΛΕΩΣ~ΑΝΤΙΟΧΟΥ~ΕΥΕΡΓΕΤΟΥ, 1931,0406.443 (Max diam. 14mm)

3.01 Bronze coin of Herod I (40 BC-4BC), minted at Jerusalem, with legend ΒΑCΙΛ ΗΡω (of King Herod) around anchor and reverse of two cornucopias, 1908,0110.302. (Max diam. 16mm)

3.02 Bronze coin of Herod I (40 BC-4BC), minted at Jerusalem, with legend ΒΑΣΙΛΕΩΣ ΗΡΩΔΟΥ (of King Herod). 1908,0110.276: X surrounded by diadem, while on the reverse, is a tripod table flanked by palm-branches. (Max diam. 18mm)

3.03 Bronze coin of Herod I (40 BC-4BC), as tetrarch ?40/39 BC. Legend = ΒΑΣΙΛΕΩΣ ΗΡΩΔΟΥ ΛΓ, 1882,0705.21: Tripod with ceremonial bowl (lebes) and tau-rho monogram to right, with reverse of military helmet shaped like round cap, with cheek pieces & straps; above, star flanked by two palm branches. (Max diam. 24mm).

3.04 Bronze coin of Herod I (40 BC-4BC), minted at Jerusalem, with legend, partly legible, ΒΑCΙΛ ΗΡωΔ (of King Herod), 1908,0110.320: cornucopia, with reverse of eagle, right. (Max diam. 13mm)

3.05 Bronze coin of Herod Archelaus (4 BC-AD 6), minted at Jerusalem, with legend, reading from front to back, ΕΘΝΑΡΧΟΥ ΗΡΩΔΟΥ (of the ethnarch Herod), 1908,0110.346: helmet, with bunch of grapes on reverse. (Max diam. 16mm)

3.06 Bronze coin minted at Jerusalem of regnal year 17 (LIZ) of Tiberius and legend ΤΙΒΕΡΙΟΥ ΚΑΙCΑΡΟC (of the emperor Tiberius) = AD 30-31, 1908,0110.530: Priest's lituus (curved wand), and reverse of inscription within wreath with berries. Although its inscriptions mention only the emperor it was struck by his governor Pontius Pilate (Max. diam.: 15mm)

3.07 Suite of denominations minted under Herod Antipas, tetrarch of Galilee and Peraea with Greek inscriptions (ΗΡΩΔΟΥ ΤΕΤΡΑΡΧΟΥ around palm), mint of Tiberias (ΤΙΒΕΡΙΑC, sometimes shortened, within wreath): double unit (undated), CM 1908,0110.362, unit (dated year 37 = AD 33-4), 1884,0705.6; half (undated), CM 1908,0110.355; and quarter (dated year 34 = AD 30-1), 1908,0110.356 . (Max. diams.25mm, 20mm, 14mm, 12mm)

3.08 Bronze coin of Herod Philip (4 BC-AD 34), minted at his capital Caesarea Paneas, AD 1-2, ΦΙΛΙΠΠΟΥ ΤΕΤΡΑΡΧΟΥ around bare head of Philip, right; while the reverse carries CΕΒΑC ΚΑΙCΑΡ around temple. IM Inv. No. 3651 © The Israel Museum, Jerusalem, photo by Vladimir Naikhin. (Max diam. 18mm)

3.09 Bronze coin of Herod, King of Chalcis, AD 43/44, BM 1985,1002.1: within legend ΒΑΣΙΛ ΗΡΩΔΗΣ ΒΑΣΙΛ ΑΓΡΙΠΠΑΣ Kings Herod (of Chalcis) and Agrippa I crown the emperor Claudius who stands between them. Claudius is labelled in the space below ΚΛΑΥΔΙΟΣ ΚΑΙΣΑΡ ΣΕΒΑΣΤΟΣ, while the reverse has inscription within wreath ΚΛΑΥΔΙΩ ΚΑΙΣΑΡΙ ΣΕΒΑΣΤΩ ΕΤ Γ (of the emperor Claudius Caesar, year three). (Max diam. 28mm)

3.10 Bronze coin of Herod Agrippa I (AD 37-44), minted at Jerusalem in AD 41/2 (year 6 of reign), BM 1908,0110.366: canopy with fringes within inscription ΒΑCΙΛΕωC ΑΓΡΙΠ; while the reverse has three corn-ears and carries date, [L] ς. (Max diam. 16mm)

3.11 Bronze coin of Herod Agrippa I (AD 37-44), minted at Caesarea Paneas, AD 37/8 (year 2 of reign), BM 1926,0501.5: Diademed bust of Agrippa I, right, with legend (mostly illegible) ΒΑΣΙΛΕΥΣ ΑΓΡΙΠΠΑΣ (king Agrippa), while on the reverse Agrippa II is shown riding horse, right, with legend ΑΓΡΙΠΠΑ ΥΙΟΥ ΒΑΣΙΛΕΩΣ (king Agrippa junior) with date below (not visible on this specimen), LB. (Max diam. 22mm)

4.01 View of the Plain of Jericho from the Jerusalem-Jericho Road (Frank Mason Good, 1866-7, © PEF-P-2063)

4.02a Silver tetradrachm of Ephesus from the time of Claudius (AD 41-54) and current during the riot (begun by the silversmiths with a vested interest in making pagan idols) caused by St Paul's visit to the city, 1844,0425.460.A: bare head of Claudius, left, with his name and titles, and on reverse the famous temple of Artemis, the Artemission, containing the mummy-like cult statue within. Artemis is labelled here in Latin using her Roman equivalent Diana. (Max diam. 26mm)

4.02b The great theatre at Ephesus today with view towards harbour. (Photo RA)

4.03 Suite of denominations minted at Rome during the early years of the emperor Vespasian, AD 69-71, most commenting on the first Jewish revolt: G3,RIG.97, IVDAEA aureus; 1862,0415.9, denarius, dynastic type with sons; R.10570, IVDAEA CAPTA type sestertius with Titus as Caesar (junior emperor) on obverse instead of Vespasian; 1924,0702.1, dupondius with Pax torching captured (Jewish) arms and armour; 1925,0105.151, IVDAEA CAPTA as; 1906,1103.2829 quadrans with palm tree and army standard (no imperial bust). (Max. diam.s: 19mm; 18mm; 32mm; 28mm; 28mm; 16mm)

4.04 Copper double mijt, minted at Antwerp, 1521-56 (reign of Charles V, Holy Roman Emperor (as Duke of Brabant)), CM 1870,0507.9254. (Max. diam.: 20mm)

4.05 Henry VIII silver farthing (GHB.402) from around the time of Tyndale's New Testament. First coinage series of 1509-1526, it carries the design of a portcullis and Tudor rose on cross. (Max. diam.: 10mm)

4.06 Silver denarius of Tiberius, the emperor contemporary to the ministry of Jesus. However, such coins were minted far to the west of the empire at Lugdunum (Lyon, central France). R.6195. Laureate head of Tiberius, right, and on the reverse, a female figure (sometimes identified with the emperor's mother Livia), seated right on chair, holding branch and sceptre. (Max. diam.: 18mm)

4.07 Tiberius silver tetradrachm (4-drachma), minted in Syria (possibly at Antioch) for circulation in the eastern part of the Roman Empire, 1927,0607.39: Bare head of Tiberius, right, and on the reverse, Zeus seated left, holding Nike and sceptre. (Max. diam.: 26mm)

4.08 Tiberius silver drachma minted at Caesarea, Cappadocia for circulation in the eastern part of the Roman Empire, 1979,0101.1097: Laureate head of Tiberius, right, and on the reverse Mount Argaeus, with figure of Helios on summit, holding globe and sceptre. (Max. diam.: 18mm)

4.09 Late Roman (4th or 5th century AD) bronze contorniate medallion, R.4861. Laureate head of Nero (AD 54-68), right, and the reverse shows a money-changer's booth. A table piled with coins stands beneath an archway; one figure stands behind the table and two figures at either side of it: the moneychanger and customers. (Max. diam.: 38mm)

5.01a Brass sestertius of Titus as Caesar (junior emperor) minted at Lyon, R1935,0404.7: Laureate head of Titus, right and on the reverse, a palm-tree; to left, captive standing right; to right, Judaea seated right on cuirass; both figures surrounded by arms. (Max. diam.: 35mm)

5.01b Detail from the Arch of Titus at Rome showing the triumphal procession of the loot from the Temple of Jerusalem (photo. John Williams, © BM)

5.02 Gold aureus of Titus as Caesar (junior emperor), minted in Judaea, AD 70, perhaps made from gold from the Temple of Jerusalem, G3,RIG.117. Laureate head of Titus, right, wearing aegis (gorgon cloak), and the reverse shows Concordia (= harmony) seated left, holding patera and cornucopia. (Max. diam.: 19mm)

5.03 First Jewish revolt silver coins, AD 66-70 (dated by years of the rebellion running from April to March): Shekel: around an Omer cup (for temple ritual) the Hebrew inscription reads: SHEKEL YISRAEL ALEPH 'shekel of Israel, year one (of revolt = AD 66-7)' while around three pomegranates the reverse reads YERUSHALAYIM KEDOSHA 'Jerusalem (the) holy', 1927,1219.1; half shekel: similar designs but obverse inscription HETZI

HASHEKEL SH(ANA)DALED, 'half shekel Israel year 4' (= AD 69-70), 1888,0512.27; quarter shekel: around three palm branches, REVA HASHEKEL, 'quarter shekel' and reverse noting year four , 1908,0110.8. (Max. diam.s: 22mm; 19mm; 16mm.

5.04 First Jewish revolt bronze prutah: in Hebrew: SHANAT SHTAYIM 'year 2' (= AD 67-8) around amphora with reverse of HERUT TZION 'freedom of Zion' around vine leaf, 1862,0714.28 (max diam. 17mm)

5.05 Bronze coin of Herod Agrippa II's regnal year 35: AD 94/5 with portrait of Domitian and minted at Caesarea Paneas, G.2631. Laureate head of Domitian, right, and reverse of Tyche (city-goddess) standing left on basis, wearing kalathos; holding corn-ears and cornucopia. (Max. diam.: 29.5 mm)

5.06 Brass sestertius of Nerva, minted at Rome, AD 97, R.11810. Laureate head of Nerva, right, with reverse device of a palm-tree. For inscription of legend FISCI IVDAICI CALVM-NIA SVBLATA see text. (Max. diam.: 36mm)

5.07 Two denominations of bronze coins of Aelia Capitolina under Hadrian. 1908,0110.1871: Laureate bust of Hadrian, right, draped and cuirassed and reverse of priest (?Hadrian), ploughing perimeter of the colony. 1908,0110.1872: Laureate bust of Hadrian, right, and reverse of Boar (badge of Legio X Fretensis based in the city after the fall of the temple). (Max. diam.s: 24mm; 13mm)

5.08 Bronze coin of the Second Jewish Revolt (AD 132-5), struck over Roman provincial coin of Hadrian,1908,0110.841: Hadrian's bust can still be seen (with the 'overtype' illegible) while on the other side the rebel obverse design is relatively clear: a palm tree with the name of Simon in Hebrew ŠM'WN) (Max. diam.: 28mm)

5.09 Silver zuz of the Second Jewish Revolt (AD 132-5), struck over Roman denarius of Hadrian, 1888,0512.36: Name of Simon in Hebrew ŠM'WN within wreath, and on reverse, a palm branch with Hebrew only partially visible; 'undertype' head of Hadrian, laureate, right. (Max. diam.: 19mm)

5.10 Silver sela of the Second Jewish Revolt, (AD 132-5) 1908,0110.766: Name of Simon in Hebrew ŠM'WN

around façade of the Temple of Jerusalem, and on the reverse, Hebrew slogan ('Deliverance of Jerusalem') around Jewish liturgical items: lulav and etrog. (Max. diam.: 27mm)

5.11 Brass sestertius of Hadrian, commemorating the emperor's arrival in Judaea (ADVENTVI AVG IVDAEAE), 1872,0709.587: Bare headed, draped bust of Hadrian, right. On the reverse Hadrian, raising his right hand in gesture of address and holding a scroll in his left facing Judaea, depicted as a female figure, who is sacrificing out of a patera over a lighted and garlanded altar (with victim – bull – next to it). Judaea also holds a box of incense and is flanked by children holding a palm branches. (Max. diam.: 32mm)

6.01 The House Church at Dura Europos (Eastern Syria) is the best – possibly the only – securely datable archaeological evidence of a Christian site before the official acceptance of the faith. Next to a city gate, it is in the same street as a synagogue and both must pre-date the sack and abandonment of the city in AD 256/7. (We do not know whether the Church had already closed during the reported persecutions of the AD 250s or was simply overlooked in such a remote outpost of empire.) The walls originally had frescos of narrative scenes from the New Testament but none of the symbols (tau-rho, chi-rho or cross) that came to form the staple imagery of the official Christian art in the following century. (Photo. Prof S. James)

6.02 Bronze coin of Apamea in Phrygia depicting the story of Noah and the flood, 1885,0606.284: Laureate head of Philip I (AD 244-9), right, on the reverse Noah and his wife are shown twice: on Mount Ararat and in the ark. (Max. diam.: 35mm)

6.03 Bronze coin of Neapolis in Samaria, G.4219: Laureate and cuirassed bust of Macrinus (AD 217-8), right, and on the reverse, view of Mount Gerizim crowned by temple of Zeus. (Max diam. 26mm)

6.04 Revelation 1,4-7: papyrus fragment of the 3rd or 4th century AD from Egypt, BMC 203 & 219 / Pap. 2053. The nomina sacra for Jesus Christ is visible as IH XP. © British Library Board

6.05 Silver coin of Berenike II of Egypt (267/ 266 BC – 221 BC), 1867,0701.7. Her veiled bust faces right, while the reverse shows a cornucopia flanked by caps (of the dioscuri) and accompanied by legend ΒΕΡΕΝΙΚΗΣ ΒΑΣΙΛΙΣΣΗΣ (Berenike, queen). Mintmark ☧. (Max. diam. 33mm)

6.06 Bronze coin of Decius (AD 249-251) at Maeonia, 1900,0404.45. Laureate draped and cuirassed bust of Decius, right, with reverse of Dionysos in panther chariot, left, city name (ΜΑΙΟΝΩΝ) below. Reverse legend includes the name of Aurelios Aphianos, the archon abbreviated A ☧ : ЄΠ ΑΥΡ ΑΦΦΙΑΝΟΥ Β Α ☧ Α ΤΟ Β Κ ϹΤΕΦΑΝΗ. (Max. diam. 34mm)

6.07 Bronze coin of Caracalla (AD 198-217), minted at Cyzicus, AD 214-7, 1906,1010.1. Bust, of Caracalla right, laureate, cuirassed, spear over shoulder with reverse of Hades (Pluto) seated left, holding sceptre and with Cerberus at feet, addressed by Caracalla, holding sceptre and advancing, right. The city is named below together with its status of possessing four temples to the imperial cult: ΚΥΖΙΚΗΝ ΔΙϹ ΝΕΟΚΟΡ. There is much graffiti on the obverse of the coin: to left, and right, of bust: ☧ / s | Αω; on edge below bust, PAX (retrograde). It can be translated as 'Christ, Saviour, the first and last, peace' (Max. diam. 42mm)

6.08 Green basanite bust of Germanicus Caesar (15 BC - AD 19) probably from Egypt and defaced with cross, GR1872.0605.1. (Ht. 44.5cm)

7.01 Silver coins of 6th century Italy (although under the rule of successor kingdoms to the Roman Empire they still carry the named effigy of the Byzantine emperor) showing the range of early Christian symbols which can also still be seen amongst the magnificent contemporary mosaics of Ravenna and Rome: a) named bust of Anastasius (AD 491-518) with reverse of Chi-Rho Christogram within wreath, B.12295 (mint = Rome); b) named bust of Anastasius (AD 491-518) with reverse of Iota-Chi Christogram within wreath (mint = Ravenna), 1867,0704.109; c) named bust of Justin II (AD 565-578) with reverse of tau-rho staurogram between stars and within wreath, (mint = Ticinum (Pavia)), 1904,0511.40; d) named bust of Justin II (AD 565-578) with reverse of cross on steps, B.12394 (mint = Ticinum (Pavia)). (Max diams. 13mm; 14mm; 13mm; 11mm)

7.02 Two details from Codex Sinaiticus: a) Revelations 11, 8; and b) end piece of Isaiah. © British Library Board, Add. 43725 f.68 & f.329

7.03 Gold solidus of AD 336-7, minted at Antioch, R.165: Diademed, draped, and cuirassed bust of Constantine I, right, with reverse of Victory, advancing left, holding trophy and palm. The main legend of the reverse VICTORIA CONSTANTINI AVG, is accompanied by mintmarks staurogram and LXXII (marking weight relative to the pound) in field and signature of Antioch below, SMAN. (Max diam. 21mm)

7.04 Silver medallion of Constantine I minted Ticinum, AD 315: Helmeted and cuirassed bust of Constantine, facing, holding bridle of horse and cruciform sceptre and shield. (☧ badge on front of helmet), with reverse of Constantine in military dress, shouldering trophy and addressing army. The reverse legend of SALVS REIPVBLICAE means salvation of the republic. (BM electrotype 2012,4159.1 from original in Staatliche Münzsammlung München; max. diam. 24mm)

7.05 Dedicatory mosaic inscription from the basilica at Aquileia. (Photo. D. Stuttard)

7.06 Bronze nummus of about AD 322-3, minted at Trier: laureate bust of Crispus, left, with spear and ☧ – emblazoned shield, with reverse of globe on altar. 2012,4246.216 (Max diam. 20mm)

7.07 Bronze nummus of about AD 327, minted at Constantinople, 1890,0804.11: Laureate head of Constantine, right, with reverse of Constantine's ☧-topped standard (Labarum) pierces a serpent representing his defeated rivals. (Max. diam. 18mm)

7.08 Gold solidus of AD 337 commemorating the deification of Constantine I, 1986,0610.1 (minted at Constantinople): Veiled bust of Constantine, right, with reverse of

Constantine, driving chariot right, and reaching up to grasp the hand of God, above. (Max diam. 22mm)

7.09 Bronze nummus of AD 350, minted at Siscia (nowadays Sisak near Zagrab), B.3651. diademed, draped and cuirassed bust of Vetranio (AD 350), right, with Constantine's vision illustrated on reverse as Victory crowning emperor holding Labarum and motto HOC SIGNO VICTOR ERIS (by this sign you will be victorious); mintmark of Siscia below. (Max diam. 23mm)

7.10 Bronze nummus of AD 350-3, minted at Amiens,1951,1115.2713: Bare headed, draped and cuirassed bust of Magnentius, right, with reverse of ☧-flanked by alpha and omega (AMB mintmark below). The reverse inscription (SALVS DD NN AVG ET CAES) can be translated as the salvation of our lords the emperor and Caesar (junior emperor). (Max diam. 29mm)

7.11 19th century drawing of a graffito from Rome; pagans mocking Christianity through the shameful death of crucifixion: 'Alexamenos worships his god' reads the comment (in Greek) below a figure regarding a crucified donkey-man. The language and name suggests a member of the Greek early Christian community at Rome and it is usually dated loosely across most of the pagan imperial era, i.e. 1st –3rd century AD (although there is no reason why such mockery could have continued after official toleration of the faith). The original is housed in the Palatine Antiquarium, near where it was discovered.

7.12 Bronze medallion of Helena (FLAVIA HELENA AVGVSTA), minted at Rome around the time she received the title of augusta (empress), AD 324: draped bust of Helena, right, with reverse of Pietas and children (PIETAS AVGVST[AE]), 1872,0709.430 (max diam. 39mm)

7.13 Bronze nummus of about AD 335, minted at Aquileia, B.3095: Laureate and cuirassed bust of Constantine I right, with the reverse of two soldiers each holding a standard. Mintmark of † over AQP. (Max diam. 17mm)

7.14 Bronze nummus of AD 316, minted at Ticinum, B.2829: Laureate and cuirassed bust of Constantine I right, with the reverse of Sol, radiate, standing left in gesture of ad-

dress and holding globe. Mintmarks + * in field and PT below. (Max diam. 19mm)

7.15 Gold coin of about AD 340-400, minted at Aksum, Ethiopia, 1921,0316.1: Half-length bust right, crowned, holding sceptre and flanked by corn-ears, with other side showing bust, right, wearing headcloth, holding branch and flanked by corn-ears. The legends a punctuated with crosses and may be translated as reading from the first to second side: King Ezanas ~ Of the Aksumites man of Alene. (Max diam. 15mm)

7.16 Bronze nummus minted at Cyzicus (Asia Minor), AD 404-6, 1951,1115.1276: Diademed, draped and cuirassed bust of Honorius (AD 393-423), right with reverse of cross. (Max diam. 11mm)

7.17 Ivory panel from a casket, early AD 400s, with the earliest surviving narrative depiction of the crucifixion. On the left, Judas hangs from tree; below him the purse with thirty pieces of silver; in the centre, the crucified Jesus is beardless and nimbate (haloed) and nailed by the hands only with his feet unsupported and calmly accepting his fate with no expression of pain; above him, the titulus plaque reads REX IVD(aeorum) in Latin (king of the Jews); on the right the soldier Longinus spears Christ's side; to the left of the cross stand Mary and John the Baptist (Mary and John in the presence of Jesus would go on to form a common composition in medieval art known as the Deisis). PE 1856,0623.5; h. = 75mm, w. = 98mm.

7.18 Gold solidus Aelia Galla Placidia (empress AD 421-450; coin struck in the AD 420s), R.303. Diademed and draped bust of Placidia, right, crowned by the hand of God, with reverse of Victory standing left, holding long jewelled cross. Below is mintmark of Constantinople. (Max diam. 22mm)

7.19 Gold solidus of Justin I (AD 522-527), with the first appearance of an angel as a coin type, 1946,1004.37: Helmeted and cuirassed bust of Justin facing, holding spear and shield, with reverse of an angel, facing, holding long cross and cross on globe (globus cruciger). Below is mintmark of Constantinople. (Max diam. 21mm)

7.20 Gold solidus of Heraclius (AD 610-41), minted at Constantinople showing the standing emperor flanked by his sons, each wearing a cross on their diadems and carrying a cross-topped globe (globus cruciger), with the reverse of a cross on steps and below CONOB with various other mintmarks in field. 1922,0523.4 (Max diam. 18mm)

7.21 Gold dinar of 'Abd al-Malik (AD 685-705 / AH 65-86), minted in Syria (about AD 690), showing standing emperor flanked by sons (without any crosses), with the reverse of a pole on steps. 1954,1011.1 (Max diam. 20mm)

7.22 Tondo (central panel) of a mid-fourth century AD mosaic pavement from Hinton St Mary, Dorset, 1965,0409.1. Beardless bust of Christ, facing, and superimposed on a Christogram flanked by pomegranates.

7.23 Gold solidus of Marcian (AD 450-7), Hunter coll. reg. 32543 © The Hunterian Museum and Art Gallery, University of Glasgow 2013: Helmeted, diademed and cuirassed bust of Marcian, facing, holding spear and shield, with reverse of Marcian and his empress Pulcheria, both nimbate and between them Jesus beardless and with nimbus cruciger. Below them is the mintmark for Constantinople and the main legend commemorating the imperial marriage: FELICITER NЧBTIIS. (Max diam. 22mm)

7.24 Gold solidus of Anastasius I (AD 491-518) mounted as a pendant, © Dumbarton Oaks, Byzantine Collection, Washington, DC, BZC.1959.47: Helmeted, diademed and cuirassed bust of Anastasius, facing, holding spear and shield, with reverse of Anastasius and his empress Ariadne, and between then Jesus bearded and with nimbus cruciger. Below them is the mintmark for Constantinople and the main legend commemorating the imperial marriage of AD 491: FELICITER NVbTIIS. (Max length with mount 29mm)

7.25 Gold solidi of Justinian II minted at Constantinople of his a) first (AD 685-695), and b) second (AD 705-711) reigns, 1852,0903.23 & 1918,0204.164: a) Bust of Christ, with flowing hair and beard, facing with cross behind head, in act of benediction and holding Bible (IhS CRISTVS REX REGNANTIЧM = Jesus Christ, king of kings) with the reverse of the standing emperor holding cross potent and mappa (napkin). b) similar obverse but bust shows Jesus with curly hair and shorter beard with reverse of diademed bust of Justinian II facing holding long cross and cross on globe (globus cruciger) marked PAX (peace). (Max diam.s 21mm and 20mm)

7.26 Bronze 'anonymous follis', minted at Constantinople, late 10th – early 11th centuries AD, B.12600. Bust of Christ, facing with nimbus cruciger and holding Bible, flanked by nomina sacra IC XC for Ιησους Χριστος with the reverse given over to the legend 'Jesus Christ, king of kings' (IhSЧS XRISTЧS bASILЄЧ bASILЄ). (Max diam. 30mm)

General Index